BOUNTY

BOUNTY

A Harvest of Food Lore and Country Memories
From Utah's Past

Janet Alm Anderson

PRUETT PUBLISHING COMPANY
BOULDER, COLORADO

First Edition

1 2 3 4 5 6 7 8 9

Library of Congress Cataloging-in-Publication Data

Anderson, Janet Alm, 1952–
    Bounty: a harvest of food lore and country memories from Utah's past / Janet Alm Anderson. — 1st ed.
        p.   cm.
    Includes bibliographical references and index.
    ISBN 0-87108-802-9
    1. Cookery—Utah.   2. Recipes—Utah.   I. Title.
TX715.T2565   1990   90-39737
641.59792—dc20   CIP

Cover and book design by Jody Chapel
Front cover photo: I. R. Pierce of Salem proudly displays an impressive crop of homegrown fruit. (Special Collection and Archives. Utah State University.)

CONTENTS

*For Mom and Dad
with love*

Acknowledgements

Thanks to the students, teachers, fieldworkers, and informants; keepers of notebooks, recipe files, journals, and diaries; and Utah photographers—all of whose work has gone into the making of this book. Creators of these records of our lives leave us a priceless legacy.

Thanks to Ann Buttars, Brad Cole, Bob Parsons, A. J. Simmonds, and Jeannie Simmonds of the Special Collections and Archives of Utah State University. Their patient assistance over many months has been greatly appreciated. Their ongoing efforts ensure the survival and accessibility of a significant record of Utah's cultural history.

Thanks to Peter Briggs and to Beverly Brannan and the Library of Congress Prints and Photographs Division staff for assistance acquiring Farm Security Administration photos taken in Utah by Russell Lee.

Thanks to those who shared their family recipes, notebooks, and journals with me: Sharon Allen, Nan Booth, Vera Christensen, Alta Fife, Mardyne Matthews, Edith Morgan, Miiko Toelken, and Betty Webb.

And thanks to Max Peterson, director of Utah State University's Merrill Library, for his support of this project.

A Note to the Reader

A few years ago I began to delve around in the Special Collections materials of Utah State University's Merrill Library. My reward for these explorations was story after story of the lives and struggles of earlier Utahns. The reality of their anecdotes and memories struck me. These were more revealing, more touching, more comical, and more exciting than the chapters of any history book — because they were personal, the real lives of real Utahns told in their own words.

I selected the anecdotes, recipes, and photos that follow for two reasons: because they are individually interesting and because they illustrate the variety of cultural resources available to us in Utah's archives and communities. And individually or collectively, I believe they tell us something about ourselves and about our history.

This book is the product of the time and effort and knowledge of many Utahns over many years: university student interviewers and their informants; Utahns who kept diaries, journals, or recipe notebooks; early as well as recent photographers, many of them anonymous with the passing of time. Much of the material included is from the bulletins of the Utah Agricultural Experiment Station and Extension Service. Their staffs' educational efforts have influenced generations of Utah cooks and farmers. Years of librarianship cannot be overlooked, either, in the preservation of these valuable cultural records. The source of each item can be found in the Sources section at the end of the book.

Not all the recipes and remedies here should be considered accurate or even safe by modern standards. Jotted in a notebook or given from memory to an inquiring student, some may not even be complete. But all the recipes, anecdotes, memories, beliefs, and photographs included here — so far as can be determined — are from the state of Utah, and together they form a sort of collective memory, a taste of Utah's bounty.

INTRODUCTION

On July 24, 1847, Brigham Young looked down into the Salt Lake Valley and announced, "This is the place." Young and his company had crossed the plains in search of a homeland for members of the young but growing Church of Jesus Christ of Latter Day Saints, or Mormons. Church members had already been expelled from New York, Ohio, Missouri, and Illinois. Temporarily camped along the banks of the Missouri River, they awaited word from their leader that a place for settlement had been found.

Arid and soil-poor, the Salt Lake Valley and surrounding region offered the struggling religious community relief from the suspicion and hostilities they had encountered where desirable land made for angry competition. And here the clannish cooperation, sense of mission, and religious cohesion that had caused "gentiles" to fear and attack them would be the qualities that would enable the Mormon settlers to carve an existence out of the hostile environment.

The Mormons were not independent and free-spirited pioneers looking for land to settle and subdue in the search for personal freedom. Alone against the region's scarcity of water and resources, as individuals they would probably not have survived. But they were a dedicated and well-organized community of pioneers whose survival depended on their unselfish unity of purpose. Cooperatively they cleared fields and dug irrigation canals. They worked not only for themselves, but built and plowed and planted for the Mormons who would follow them across the plains. Their goal was independence—for the group.

By 1850, when the Territory of Utah was established, the population had grown to 11,380. The early plan of a self-sufficient, agrarian-based, and cooperative society had largely been realized. The sought-after independence from religious persecution was being established through independence in food production, crafts, trades, and commerce.

Control of food production was an important step in early Mormon church efforts at self-sufficiency. Land and irrigation water were both held in common. Irrigation systems were built through the work of whole communities. A complex and well-organized church welfare system was established, and tithes were often paid in produce—food to be redistributed to members in need. Food preservation and sharing were encouraged. Self-sufficiency is a theme that has run through Mormon church activities from the first. Large families and a farming lifestyle have encouraged preservation and storage of foodstuffs. Even today the Mormon church encourages each family to maintain a year's supply of food for emergency use.

Although self-sufficiency and independence from other religious groups were the goals, early settlers no sooner began to make progress at establishing their isolated frontier community than they found themselves at the crossroads of an expanding nation. In 1849 gold was discovered in California, and a rush of would-be miners trekked across the Mormon territory and found Salt Lake City a welcome opportunity for rest and trade. Suddenly a stop on the main route of miners and westbound emigrants, the Mormons had food and livestock to trade for the household goods, clothing, and furniture they had been unable to bring on their own crossing of the plains. Business boomed for farriers and metalworkers who served the horseshoeing and repair needs of the travelers.

As the gold rush subsided, emigrants bound for California and Oregon kept the outside trade alive, and some stopped to settle among the Mormons, adding their skills and trades to the economy of the region. The controlled self-sufficiency of the earliest times began to break down as new products and new possibilities for trade became available. Eighteen sixty-nine brought the transcontinental railroad, and with it came access to new markets as well as to new products. Utahns were beginning the change from a localized agrarian-based economy to a system of industrial producers and cash consumers. A preference for imported furniture, carpets, wallpaper, and other outside goods over locally produced products emerged.

The development of trade with outside suppliers and consumers encouraged cultural diversification—the development of manufacturing and an influx of outsiders. And the Mormon church itself, through its diligent missionary work, was bringing cultural diversity into its own population at an enormous rate. During the 1800s, 80,000 Latter Day Saints arrived in Utah to settle after their conversion to the Mormon faith. They came from the nations of Great Britain and Scandinavia as well as from other parts of Europe, the Middle East, the Far East, and even the Pacific islands. With this growth the church worked vigorously to expand its territory, sending out selected groups of farmers and tradesmen to establish as many as 400 communities by the turn of the century.

Non-Mormon immigrants arrived, too: Irish and Chinese to build the railroads; Irish, Welsh, Finns, and Swedes to work in the growing mining industry; Japanese, Koreans, and Mexicans in agricultural industries; and southern Europeans, Greeks, Armenians, Croatians, Serbs, and others to apply their labor to the mining and railroad operations. A Native American population survived the white incursion and remains part of the state's population today.

Vestiges of this early immigrant diversity remain. In Cache Valley, for example, older residents can still recite the original ethnic affiliation of each town in the valley—which was the English town, the Swiss, the Welsh, and so on.

In the last decades of the nineteenth century, however, the Mormon church's and the Territory of Utah's desire for acceptance, integration, and statehood grew, and an emphasis on cultural homogenization and Americanization emerged. With growing official acceptance, modernized transportation and communications helped to increase the influence of the American popular culture of the day—from publications like ladies' magazines to products like canned oysters and margarine.

When the Utah Agricultural College, a land grant institution, was established in 1888, educational efforts by the college and the extension service also helped homogenize the culture of the state. Educators worked to standardize agricultural and household practices across the state with scientific information from across the nation. Modern and efficient farming techniques were advocated. Safer and more efficient food preservation was taught, and nutritious recipes were disseminated.

Today Utah's food traditions are as fully Americanized as those of Ohio or Massachusetts. Utahns watch pizza advertisements on television and try out recipes from *Ladies Home Journal*. They shop at the same chain grocery stores as shoppers in Florida and Oregon, and they grab a quick meal at Burger King.

Still, Utah is a young state (statehood was granted less than 100 years ago), and Utahns don't have to reach very far back into memory when they enjoy Navajo fry bread at a county fair or savor a community sauerkraut dinner in a town founded by Swiss immigrants. The diversity of Utah's food heritage lingers, enriching the fares of the state's tables.

BOUNTY

CLIMATE

Well, I think the climate is—it's been a kind of strain on the people's faith because they have to have a lot of faith to plant anything in this country. And if it freezes this year, they figure it'll be a better year next, and so they go and plant it again next year. But I think that we do live in a wonderful country. We've got a lot of things to be thankful for. We've got a lot of good things to be thankful for. We've got a lot of good things—a lot of good beef and lamb and so forth. And I think that we can't stay here because of the climate. I guess we have to stay here in spite of it.

J. Earl Stuart
Randolph

HARVESTERS' BREAKFAST

Some mornings it was foggy. You couldn't put up hay until noon. You had to wait for the hay to dry. In the afternoon it would get hot, up in the 90's, and yet when you'd get up in the mornings, it was so cold I wore flannel pajamas to bed. I'd get up in the morning and put some of those blue striped bib overalls we used to wear and a flannel shirt over the top of my pajamas and go out in this old shack and cook breakfast for the men. I would cook breakfast, and you know, hay men work hard. It was such hard work that you had to give them steak for breakfast. These puny breakfasts we have now days wouldn't go very far. Anyway, we'd have to cook steak for breakfast if you can imagine. So I'd have to get up about 5:00 in the morning in order to have it ready.

Bernice Weston Sims

"Mormon farmer at noon-day dinner." Box Elder County, August 1940. (Photo by Russell Lee for Farm Security Administration, Library of Congress.)

PORKCHOPS

My father worked his way across the country. And like I said, he was a little hurt because he couldn't speak English. He talked about how he got on a train and he didn't know what to order to eat. He heard a fellow say "porkchops," so he ate porkchops all the way across the U.S.A.

Katherine J. Vilos

PORK SAUSAGE

For sausage we'd use a little bit of this and a little bit of that, salt and pepper and sage. And pork. You just have to season it just right. We used to have sort of a recipe we followed. I don't remember it now. There was salt and pepper and sage, and there was some other flavoring you put in, but I can't remember. It's been a long time ago. Then these little white sacks that salt used to come in. They'd be about that long. We'd wash them up and stuff them full of sausage. The old salt sacks. And then we didn't have a freezer, so we'd hang them on the north side of the house, and there they'd freeze all winter. Outside on the outside of the wall. We'd keep them up high, and they'd stay there all winter.

Stanley and Esther Morgan
Logan

SUCKLING PIGS

He didn't get very much per pound out of [suckling pigs]. I don't remember. It'd be somewhere between seven and eight cents a pound. Something like that. The most we ever got for a big pork, like I said earlier, was three cents a pound on foot, and that didn't bring much profit.

Harry Lunn
Ogden

PICKLING PIGS' FEET

The feet are well scraped, and the toe nails and dew claws are removed. The feet are placed in a kettle, covered with water, and cooked until tender, which will require about 5 hours. Salt, to suit the individual taste, is added to the water while cooking. When the feet are tender, they are split with a knife and packed in an earthen jar covered with hot vinegar; spices are added.

Utah State Agricultural College
Agricultural Experiment Station
1929 (#80)

HARD TIME DANCE

We used to have the "hard time" dances down there, and every year they would have a "hard time" dance. People would bring produce instead of their tickets. One night a fellow brought a little pig and turned it loose. The little pig ran around in the hall nearly all night about scared to death. I guess he could not imagine what was happening.

Lydia Ann Taylor Skewes
Moab

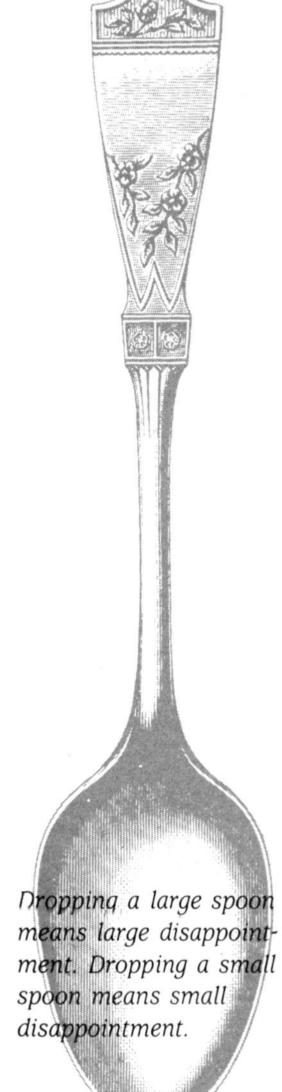

Dropping a large spoon means large disappointment. Dropping a small spoon means small disappointment.

Hogs catch the attention of the "farm wife" at the recreated 1917 Jensen Living Historical Farm. Wellsville, 1986. (Photo by Jeannie Thomas. R. V. Jensen Living Historical Farm.)

7 ॐ

HELP ON SNOWSHOES

So this here one day just before Christmas, why, I killed two pigs, and I got my neighbor to help me. And my oldest boy was ten, so he helped a little. The next morning I had erysipelas. I couldn't get out of bed, and I had two pigs strung up. I was lying there, and finally, along about noon, my wife could see someone come up across the field on snowshoes. She told me we was going to have company. She said someone was coming up here on snowshoes. When he got up here, it was our good friend from Holbrook. He drove a team of sleighs up to my neighbors', and he stopped there. He said the road looked pretty rough up to there, so he would leave his team there and walk. I said, "Well, you sure come just when I wanted to see you." He was a good singer, and he'd been on a mission. We visited for a while, and then I told him what I had. He said, "Well, I'll soon have them in the brine for you." I had the barrel all fixed up, and he wanted to know how to make the brine, so I told him how to make the brine, and he made the brine. And that night he had both pigs in the barrel and in the brine. Then he sang to us. He was a good singer. He stayed with us that night and sure enjoyed himself. I don't know what I'd have done if he hadn't come. I would have probably lost my pigs. I told him that. He said, "Oh, whatever I done, I was happy. I just wanted to see you, and I thought the only way to see you was to come up to your place." And I sure did enjoy having him there that night.

Pierce Hardman
North Logan

A young shepherd watches over his charges, a flock of
Rambouillet sheep, in 1903. (Special Collections and Archives.
Utah State University.)

Shipping by Rail

The lambs, like I say, were earlier in the season, and for three years the boss just about topped the market. He'd ship some years to Duluth and some years to Chicago. I started out with him once, and I made it as far as Ogden here. That was enough for me. I got off and walked out to my—I got relatives here in south Weber. I went out there and stayed with them awhile. In those days they had them old time brakes, and the connections on the freight cars was just a big loop. That was a lot of slack. When he put on the brakes, then the cars'd jam, and the sheep, a lot of them would smother. The only thing you could do was open the doors and throw them out. Nothing else you could do about them to save the carcass or anything of that kind. You'd just have to climb down there and open that door and go in and gather out the dead ones and then climb out the door and get up on top of the car and go back to the crummy caboose.

Harry Lunn
Ogden

Spring Lambing

I was born and raised in Manti, and my father was a sheep man. And I would go with him up on the hills with him sometimes during the spring lambing. And any little lambs, Dad'd bring them home and put them out on the back coal porch.

Shirley M. Griffin
Brigham City

DOCKING LAMBS

For years and years, for many years, we would dock the lambs. We usually docked them—the operation consisted of putting your ear marks on them and also cutting their tail off. With wethered lambs you'd cut the tail so it was short. Then with the wether lambs, you'd castrate them. And for many, many years, we would use our teeth for pulling the testicles. Of course, that's kind of a bloody operation. I was glad when we didn't have to do that, but I did much of that. Well, my wife says, "That's difficult to have you go out and do that and then you come home and you want to kiss me."

A. J. Anderson
Fairview

SHEEPHERDER'S GIFT

No, we never had any mutton. Oh, once in a while there would be a sheepherder come through. They used to take sheep to the canyons from different places, and they would move them through and pass in front of our place. And they'd stop, and Mother would always seem to have pie ready for any stranger that came along the road. I remember one time an old sheepherder gave us a lamb because of the pie that Mother had baked for him and took out to his little sheep camp.

Sarah Wyatt Leishman
Nibley

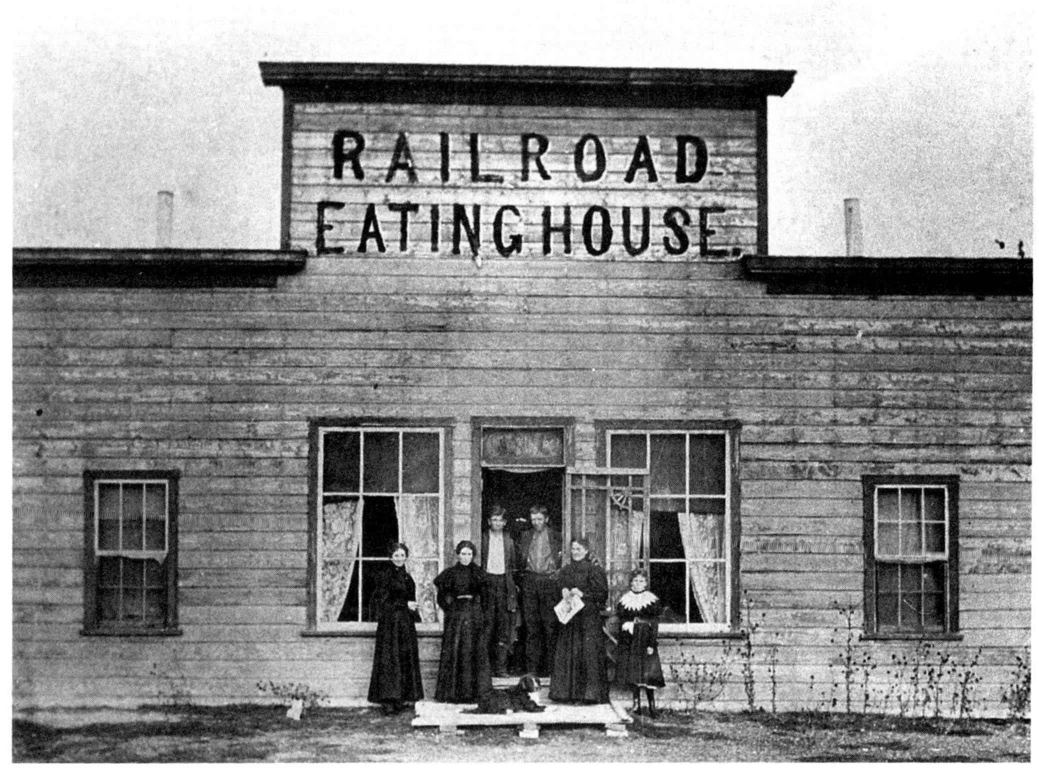

The Railroad Eating House served Cache Junction and the railroad trade about 1900. (Special Collections and Archives. Utah State University.)

DEPRESSION RENT

Well, if you had 15¢ you could get a couple of pounds of hamburger, or you could get two dozen eggs. A lot of times we never had the 15¢. We had to go work for it. In fact, I hauled wood down from the mountains. Sister Flo Moss, who I was renting off from at the time for $8 a month — and I couldn't find any $8, so she said, "You bring me a load of wood and cut it up, and I'll take it from there." That's the way we got through the winter.

Lester Knighton
Bountiful

BEARS

We socialized somewhat with the other [sheep] herders from outfits that we knew like these Bowden brothers and different ones like that. These Bowden brothers, the bears had been bothering them. They had the tent below a little shallow canyon. One brother slept in the tent, and the other brother took a bed up here. Well, the bears got in. It was a moonlight night, and in the dusk they couldn't see what happened, so they both climbed trees. Well, it come towards daylight, and the bears had left. They'd killed several sheep and raised hob. This one up in the tree, he could see [the other] up in the tree down here and figured that was another bear. They was scared. Finally they hollered back and forth and got down. Well, that scared them so that they wouldn't sleep like that again. They both slept in the tent, and the bears got into them again. The one, the older brother, he got up and grabbed the rifle. He thought he seen a bear right out in front of the tent in the dark, and he shot at it. They'd hung their [Dutch oven] in the tree and put a blanket over it. He blowed that all to pieces. Yes, he thought it was a bear.

Harry Lunn
Ogden

Cattle Guard

One of the best stories I ever heard took place there while I was on his ranch. He had a cowboy named Chet Smith that didn't believe in progressive new-fangled things. Among the things Chet used to laugh at was me because I was such an awkward horseman. I had leased Charlie's dairy herd, so I didn't need to be a good cowboy. But Charlie read in the farm magazine somewhere that if you took a piece of hardtop road, blacktop road, and painted a cattle guard on it, that calves and cows would think that was a cattle guard and not walk across it. So right on that road between the junction and La Sal, which was still dirt, he had about a hundred yards—maybe less than that—blacktopped. Then right in the middle of that he pinched it in just like a real cattle guard comes and painted that cattle guard on there. It wasn't long until cattle were getting out and going out on the highway and getting killed. One day I came tootling along there in my old Plymouth, and there was a great big sign on a piece of cardboard with a stick there that said, "Cows, Please Note—This is a Cattle Guard." Old Chet Smith, the long time cowboy, had run that sign up there, and I got about as big a bang out of that as anything I ever saw.

David Sharp

WINTER OUTHOUSE

Yes, you get out there at night, boy, you take a scoop and a shovel and broom and everything to go to the bathroom. . . . And all you got to do [now] is push on a button to go to the bathroom. All that shoveling was crazy. Broom—to sweep the snow off! You didn't want to sit there in the snow. Cold, boy!

Pierce Hardman
North Logan

GEESE

We had some geese there that gave the boys a lot of problems. I remember one day we had our own gander that was very possessive of his females, and the boys had been up in the pastures, way up in the east of our place. I saw them coming down through the field and running just as fast as they could come. When I went out to see what was the matter, the old gander was right behind them, and he had hold of one of their shirt tails. As they were running he was just riding along. They were frightened to death of him.

Eva Mae Israelson
North Logan

Women are trained to pluck turkeys in a poultry processing plant, Tremonton, c. 1946. (Utah State University Photo Services.)

Measles Remedy

When a child has been exposed to measles and is having difficulty breaking out, the following remedy is offered:

1. Place a dead chicken with its feathers on in a large pot and boil it for two hours or until the child breaks out.
2. If this does not work, feed the child the broth water.

Banty Rooster

We had a small chicken coop. We had an old banty rooster that hated me, and I couldn't go in the chicken coop without that banty sitting up on top just waiting for me. And one day he got me. I couldn't see him anywhere around, and all of a sudden here he was on top of my head. We had him for dinner that night.

Shirley M. Griffin
Brigham City

The Accumulation of Money
Not the Aim of Existence

This is the day of labor saving devices in the home as well as on the farm. Scarcely any man would deny their place on the farm, because he sees in their use the saving to him in dollars and cents, and that always makes a strong appeal, since upon his success depends the welfare of the entire family. If a sixty dollar mowing machine will enable him to cut as much grass in one hour as his father cut in one day with a scythe, the argument is complete, and he will have it if he has to mortgage the farm to get it. But if a sixty dollar vacuum cleaner would enable his wife to do as much cleaning in one hour as her mother did in one day, he would doubtless spend many months thinking about the expenditure of the sixty dollars. Again, this is not necessarily because the man is hard-hearted, unfeeling, or stingy, but because, if he thought of it at all, he would feel that man is the bread-winner; through his labors the money and the wherewithal of life come into the home, and any expenditure is justified therefore. But is money the end of existence? What good is a large bank account to any man if he has the consciousness of a wornout, ill-tempered wife and a cheerless home to greet him when his day's work is done? And no woman whose energy is taxed to the breaking point by the ceaseless daily, and often nightly, grind of toil can be companionable for any length of time. Is there a money equivalent for the cheerful smile and life companionship of the woman who was once the best on earth? Can money pay for the lack of things? Sometimes money does pay — it often pays coffin bills and undertaker's fees; and many a man has found that one hospital bill or doctor's fee would have bought many a vacuum cleaner. Is it not better to practice the ounce of prevention method? The farmer who understands that there are things in life worth infinitely more than dollars and cents will use every spark of intelligence and some hard cash as well in making the most perfect possible home.

Utah Agricultural College Experiment Station
Extension Division
1912 (#6 [7?])

THANKSGIVING DAY 1895

This is Thanksgiving Day. I spent the day at home. Asahel & Ovando C. Beebe joined with the 100 Men who went to Camp Floyd to shoot Rabbits for the poor. Asahel got 26 Ovando 35. The whole Company got 1,800 Rabbits. Asahel lost his $10 gold spectacles and one Man Lost a gold watch. There was 2 or 3 inches of Snow on the Ground. I received another letter from Owen to Father Mother Blanche & Alice.

Wilford Woodruff

Woodruff entered the Salt Lake Valley with the first company of Mormon settlers in 1847. From 1889 to 1898 he served as fourth president of the Mormon church. As church president he issued the Manifesto of 1890, discontinuing the practice of polygamy.

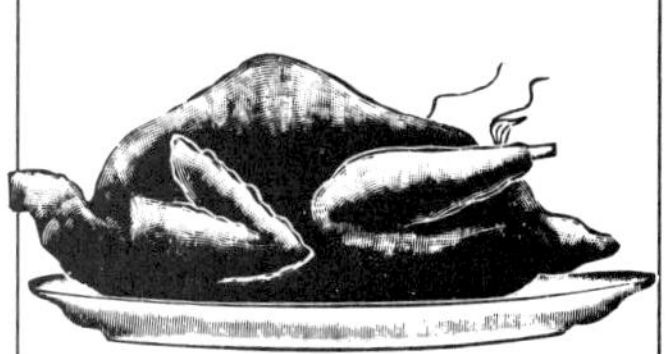

PRAIRIE DOGS AND FLOUR

When I come out here, we didn't have hardly anything to go on, had a pretty rough time of it. Some people went kind of hungry at times, and one feller told me, he said he moved out from Colorado, and he said he never had anything but a sack of flour and lived on prairie dogs all summer.

John Spencer
Fort Duchesne

Sing at the table,
Whistle in bed,
The devil will get you
As soon as you're dead.

This winter jackrabbit round-up occurred in northern
Sanpete County in 1912. (Special Collections and Archives.
Utah State University.)

20

Rabbit Burrow

As a whole the Indian was pretty well to do as far as game. He could go out and get it any time he wanted it. There wasn't any restrictions on it, although he might of had a hard time getting his rabbits. A lot of people didn't own guns, and they had to go get them the best way they could. . . . I remember going out with an uncle one time, where we could run him to the end of his trail, and finally we would take a piece of barb wire. We'd take this barb wire. Oh, it would be about an eight or ten foot piece of barb wire. The ends would kind of be flared out at the edges. So what we'd do is take it and screw this length of the wire down in the rabbit's burrow and entangle the barb wire into the rabbit's fur. This is the way we'd pull him out of his hole. This is how we would manage to get our dinner. It really wasn't what you would call a real happy life. It was hard.

LaMar LaRose

Magpies

Well, I'll tell you. We had a lot of chickens. We had a coop, but we couldn't keep them shut up all the time, so we just let them run loose. A lot of them would go up in the hay loft and lay their eggs there. The eggs that I gathered up there were for Mother, and she enjoyed that because she could exchange them at the store for things that she wanted. Sometimes when I'd go to gather the eggs, I'd find empty shells with the eggs sucked out. Or broken or cracked eggs and a lot of feathers. We discovered that the magpies were flying in there and doing the damage. As a result, Mother wasn't getting her share of the eggs.

One day I saw advertised in the newspaper — the folks were gone for three or four days — where you could get some strychnine for rodents at the courthouse in small amounts. But you'd have to come there and certify what you wanted it for and so on. It was restricted. So I got out my horse, hitched up, and rode to the courthouse. I got a little package of strychnine.

A few days before, Dad had killed a hog, and Mother had the liver in our ice box. I whacked off a little piece of that liver and climbed up the ladder and nailed the liver to the top of a corral post. I took out my pocket knife and cut a few slits in the liver and then poured in the strychnine.

We had about eight hogs in that corral. I went out the next day, and those hogs were laying around dead, I thought. I kicked them, and they wouldn't move. I put my foot on them — no sign or sound, but I thought I could see their bodies moving a little. Then I concluded that that was because I was pushing them. But then I saw those feathers. It looked like tons and tons of them, exaggerating a bit, but there were feathers everywhere. Then I realized what had happened. Those magpies had eaten the strychnine, fallen into the corral, and then the hogs ate the poisoned magpies.

When Dad came home I took him out to the corral. "Something happened," I said. I explained about the magpies. He didn't say I had done a good job of getting rid of the magpies. He said, "That was pretty risky." I asked, "What about the pigs?" "Oh," he said, "don't worry about the pigs. They've got at least an inch of fat clear around their bodies, and you couldn't kill a pig with strychnine. They'll be all right, all of them."

A herd of Hereford beef cattle grazes under cowboys' supervision in 1956 as a locomotive passes in the background. (Special Collections and Archives. Utah State University.)

It wasn't long until those pigs came alive, all of them. But you know, we never had another magpie flying in that barn. Every magpie in this valley must have known about that.

Joseph H. Watkins, Jr.

BEDTIME

My older brother Raleigh always played the mandolin. When we built the new house I remember we'd go to bed, of course, when it was time, and he'd sit there and play the mandolin for us to sleep by. We used to have just a lot of fun.

Eva Campbell Bybee
Providence

HEADCHEESE

We made headcheese. Headcheese out of the pig's head. Put that pig head on and cook it and then dig out the meat, the good meat out of it after and some of the fat. And it was mixed with your sage, salt, and pepper. And when it was all cooked, you molded it into loaves, and you'd slice it off. Mold it just with your hands. Shape it with your hands, you know, into these molds. Then you'd put it down in your cellar because there was not refrigeration then. And put it down in your cellar. And that's where we had to keep things. Wrap it, but then they didn't have the paperware, you know. It would be in cloth. It stayed fresh because

*"F.S.A. cooperative tractor." Box Elder County, August 1940.
(Photo by Russell Lee for Farm Security Administration,
Library of Congress.)*

our cellar was built down under the ground. And it had a dirt floor, and the lower down you'd get, the colder it would be.

Maxine Rawlins
Cove

Hickory Smoking

Then Grandfather and Brother Shelby were called by the church authorities to come up here and settle in Laketown and Randolph, and Grandfather Satterthwaite's old home still stands here. When he came from Indiana, he brought with him a recipe for curing ham and bacon and side pork and so on, and each year he would butcher three or four good hogs. He had plenty of feed for them. Then he had the little smokehouse, and a friend of his in Indiana would ship him a cord of hickory wood, and he would take a team and go to Salt Lake City and haul that hickory wood to Laketown to cure his meat. We had some of the best pork sausage I have ever eaten, and in those days, Grandmother used to make the coverings, or the casings, as they used to call them, for the sausage by sewing cheesecloth and stuffing it with sausage. Then she would dip it in mutton tallow and let it set until the tallow hardened so it would help preserve the sausage.

Vella Satterthwaite
Laketown

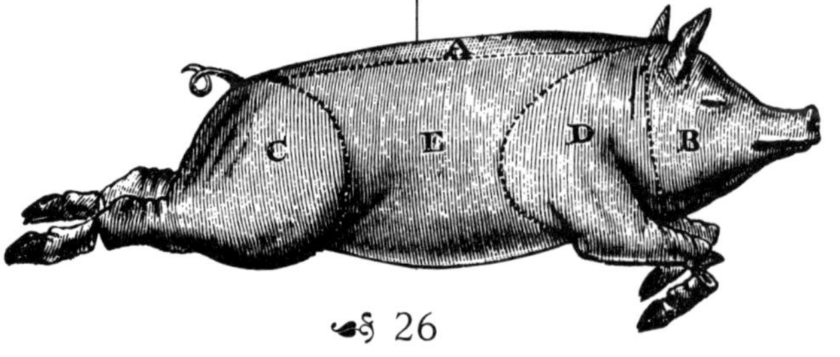

HOG DRIVE

In the fall of the year all of the men raised pigs—hogs, they called them. I remember Father had such a big herd. In the fall they couldn't sell them around here, so they would count the heads of pigs each farmer had, and they would drive them in the road. The Wyatts, the Woods, the Browns, and the Greens, and all of them down there. They had men on each side of the road. They would have them in the road and drive them up there. They were taken by rail to Ogden and sold. Some were big hogs, and some were little ones. They were different sizes, mothers and some fathers. So when they got the money back, they paid each farmer according to the number of hogs they had. I remember when Father came in with his little old leather sack and his money, it was all in gold pieces. They paid them in gold pieces. It wasn't silver, nickels and dimes. We didn't know what that was. But it was gold pieces.

Annie Leishman
Wellsville

CLEANLINESS

"Dirty as a pig" is a comparison which may be true generally, but pigs are dirty because men force them to be. People would also be dirty if they were forced to spend all their time in one small room. Give a hog that has not been badly trained a sensible roomy pen and note the care with which he "keeps house."

Utah Agricultural College
Extension Division
1918 (#12)

Farmers listen as a county extension agent offers the latest information on raising beef cattle, c. 1937. (Special Collections and Archives. Utah State University.)

Indian Powwow

Soon after they lived in Laketown, why the Indians came in there one summer. Of course, the Indians had the south end of the lake because of the fishing, the deer in the mountains, and the sage chickens, and the ducks and the geese along in the valley there. The Indians didn't want to give up that territory to the white people. So they moved in there and had a great powwow one summer, somewhere between three and four thousand Indians. Of course, the word got out to President [Brigham] Young and then President Rich, who was president of the stake at that time. They got together, and they said they would have to feed the Indians and be friendly to them or they wouldn't have no chance at all. The Indians would just wipe them out. So my father, along with the rest of them, furnished an old oxen that he had. I don't know whether it was the oxen that he drove across the plains and still had it, but he furnished this oxen. If it was the one they drove across the plains, why then it would be a pretty tough old oxen.

Ray Lamborn

Cattle Competition

He told me once he was out rounding up some cattle and they'd hired somebody to come and kill him. This guy came out to kill him. They sat around the campfire talking. He ate supper with him. When he got up to leave, he told Papa that he'd come to kill him, but he decided he was a lot better man than the ones who'd hired him, so didn't.

Barbara Izatt

Jerky

Cut red meat (beef or game animals) along the grain with a sharp knife as thin as possible. Strip off all fat, sprinkle with salt and pepper, string strips on galvanized wire, cover with netting, and hang to dry for approximately one week.

Daniel Winder
Springdale

Indian School

A lot of the children had to stay at the [Uintah Indian School]. Of course, as far back as I can remember—now this goes back into the Depression days. The bigger share of the students had to live at this school because during the Depression money wasn't as readily available. And even if it was available, it wasn't of much value to anybody. So it was either go to this boarding school and at least have clothes on your back and something to eat or probable starvation. I guess it was pretty hard on the parents.

LaMar LaRose

Trading

Now we talked about high wages and low wages, but everybody was busy. And everybody had good clothes and plenty to eat. They traded pigs for sheep, traded turkeys for a pig, a horse for a couple of cows or three cows, or a cow for a couple of horses depending on what they were. They were out of the stream of the commercial world.

Ross Bartlett
Salt Lake City

A lecture train from the Agricultural College of Utah carried speakers and exhibits on a tour of Utah and Idaho in 1904. (Special Collections and Archives. Utah State University.)

SHEEP CAMP SUPPLIES

There was a fellow, Billy White, run the blacksmith shop at Woodland, and Jones owned the store. So I took my horses there to have them shod, and I went over to the store to give them my list of stuff that I wanted [for the sheep camp]. And there was several women and a bunch of children there in the store. This man Jones, a big redheaded curly-haired monster of a man, he must've weighed 230 pounds, all man, he was sitting up there playing with this blonde woman. A blonde, young woman, and sitting on the counter there. I gave him the list, and I went back to the blacksmith shop. Billy says, "What are they doing over to the store?" "Well," I says, "the Relief Society must be there. I think they are having some kind of a sewing bee." He says, "The Relief Society? That was his wives. And that young one that he was playing with, that was his latest acquisition." He had six of them. I don't know how many children, but he had a group of big, redheaded girls there. The boss had sent salt out in 150-pound bags, and just imagine, I carried 300 pounds of salt to the horse. And the boss thought that would help by sending it in two sacks instead of three, but the three was fine. You'd put one on each side and one in between. But with them two 150-pound sacks, my gracious. I realized that the lashing would cut through them sacks, so I put a piece of canvas first over, but in trying to get them sacks up here long enough to lash them to the trees was a problem, and those big, redheaded girls standing there laughing about it. I'm kind of shy anyway. I was ready to throw rocks at them.

Harry Lunn
Ogden

The Amount Required to Feed and Clothe One Soldier for One Year

Figures of the Quartermaster General, Washington, D.C.:

Beef, 456¼ lbs.
Flour, 416⅞ lbs.
Baking Powder, 2 lbs.
Beans, 54¾ lbs.
Potatoes, 456¼ lbs.
Prunes, 29.2 lbs.
Coffee, 25.51 lbs.
Sugar, 73 lbs.
Milk, 61.4 lbs.
Vinegar, 7.3 quarts
Salt, 14.6 lbs.
Pepper, 9.1 lbs.
Cinnamon, 5½ lbs.
Lard, 14.6 lbs.
Butter, 11.4 lbs.
Syrup, 14.6 lbs.
Flavoring Extract, 5¼ oz.
Cotton, 30.7 lbs.
Wool, 51.9 lbs.
Upper Leather, 23.5 square feet
Sole Leather, 14 lbs.

In addition, it is estimated from purchases made by men at the various camps that a soldier could use 120 lbs. of candy during the year.

Utah Agricultural College
Extension Division
1918 (#30)

"Two young turkey growers weigh in their birds before choosing marketable toms and hens." (Utah State Agricultural College. Extension Service. Bulletin, 1937?)

TURKEY SHOOT

He was out to this turkey shoot, and they would stick the turkeys' heads up through a box, and you was to shoot at their heads. And if you hit them in the head, well, you got the turkey. Had to pay a dime for a shot. Nobody around there much was hitting them. They was quite a ways away when they were shooting. Walter's son says, "Well, give me a crack at it." And he shot five turkeys out of six shots, and they wouldn't let him shoot anymore. And he says, "Well, I'll go get Dad. He's an old man, and maybe you can get a few dimes off of him." So Walter went out there to the turkey shoot, and they stuck the turkeys' heads up through the box, and he shot six out of six. And they stopped him. They wouldn't let him shoot anymore.

Marvin Barney
Ogden

ROAST ANTELOPE

We'd have roast leg of antelope, and I can remember the ribs. We used to particularly like the roasted ribs. The meat is a great deal like mutton. It isn't like deer meat. It's more like mutton. I'll never forget, they laid one of the hides down alongside my bed, and I was tickled about it, you see, and I jumped out of bed and lit on it. I jumped, too. That old hair was so stiff.

Harry Lunn
Ogden

Duck Limit

I didn't hunt. In the first place, I didn't have any money to buy shells or a weapon. And I didn't have time. But there were several families that did a lot of hunting. Some of them shot for the market. There was no limit at first. They shot all they could carry home. Fifty, I think, was the first limit for ducks.

Vernon Ward
Ogden

Preserving Venison

When Dad and the boys'd go out and get their deer, Dad would hang the deer and cure it. And then they'd strip it, and Mother'd can venison. And we'd have venison and venison gravy all winter long with our roasts and everything else. She had an old cooker that Dad put out in the ground. He dug a big hole in the ground just like Dutch oven cooking, and the meat would cook for some twenty-four hours down in this, and he'd keep it hot. So, but it was tightly covered. Then it would sit another twenty-four hours, and it would be taken out and cooled. Then you'd put it in glass jars and take it down in the root cellar and keep it all winter. Just keep it cool.

Shirley M. Griffin
Brigham City

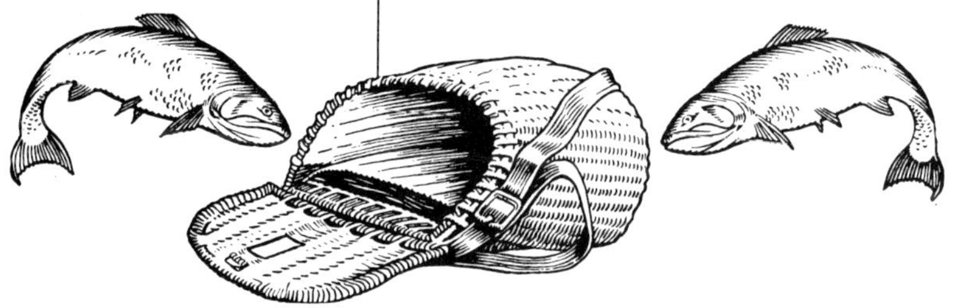

"A County Agent explains to farmers the provisions of a Federal Program." (Utah State Agricultural College. Extension Service. Bulletin, 1937?)

GAME WARDEN

The old fishermen, some of them lived in town, and they would go up to the head of the creek and do a little fishing. The game warden, he thought he'd catch these old guys. I don't know who it was or who the story was told about, but they had a board across Big Creek. And the fellow that done the fishing, he figured that the game warden would be coming. So he went out and cut this board half way through and turned it over. It held him all right going over, but when the game warden come after him, he turned it over the other way, and the bottom part that held him all right going over gave way about the time the game warden started to cross. He took a douse in the creek. Now, that's just a story that I was told. I don't know how true it was, but the fishing, we didn't know but a very little about it at that time. People were too busy to fish like they do now.

Ray Lamborn

DEER TRACKS

In them years from 1907 until 1912 was some of the hardest, the most severe winters that this country ever witnessed. They were nearly all hard winters. They did lots of damage, made awful severe hardships. There was so much heavy snow with cold weather and late springs that it wiped out practically all wildlife that was in this country. I never seen a live deer until after I was twenty-one years old. I never seen a bobcat or any of that type of wildlife until later than that. No, there was no deer. There was just coyotes and wolves and that type of stuff here up until then. When I was around twenty-one, we used to go to the canyon, and we'd see deer tracks. We was more excited over one of them deer tracks than they are now if they see a herd of deer with a thousand in it, because they were wiped out.

Loran Jackson

FISH FRY

July 24, or Pioneer Day, is celebrated in Utah as the anniversary of the first Mormon settlers' arrival in 1847.

In the summertime for the 4th and the 24th [of July] we'd always go up the canyon. All the ladies would fry fish. They'd take their frying pans right with them and build a fire and fry the fish right there and eat it right there. They'd set big long tables on the ground, on the grass. They'd fish in the stream and fry what they caught. They'd always make salads. Different kinds of salads—green salads and potato salad. We used to have a lot of fun. Usually we'd have some kind of fruit for dessert. And they would usually get lemons and make lemonade. They'd have glasses, you know. We didn't have any store cups. The ladies would just all take their glasses. We'd have the tables just as even as we could, and they'd always lay a big quilt down and spread a big tablecloth on it. Sometimes fifty people would go. They'd come from all over, you know, down on the flat. Just friends and neighbors.

Eva Campbell Bybee
Providence

BAIT

In order to catch fish, you must first use a red worm hooked on the hook in only two places. You must then spit on the worm and talk to the fish in the creek, saying, "Fish, fish, in the brook, come and nibble on my hook." It sounds silly, but it usually works.

BLACK WALT

They called him Black Walt because he didn't take a bath very often. But he was a great old boy. They was sitting around the campfire cooking beans. They had these great big pots that they would cook beans in for the soldiers. That seemed to be the main source of food was beans at that time. And even beans was scarce, so they just put a few beans in a lot of water and made soup, bean soup. And Walter was rolling up his sleeves one night, and they says, "What you going to do, Walt?" He says, "I'm going to dive in that pot and see if I can find a bean."

Marvin Barney
Ogden

PEANUT BUTTER SOUP

Use one tablespoon peanut butter for each cup of thin white sauce. A little freshly cut parsley sprinkled over the top makes a very attractive soup.

U.S.A.C. Extension Service
1948 (#170)

*Flowers grace this dinner table at which the photographer may
be the fourth diner, for whom the extra place is set, c. 1917.
(Special Collections and Archives. Utah State University.)*

Green Soup

To purify the blood in Spring. Use the little green sprouts from the garden.

Boil diced potatoes in a little water.
Add cut up green onions—including the green tops.
Add chopped fresh caraway.
Add milk.

Mary Jacobsen Sorensen
Mendon

Pop Corn Soup for 50

3 gallons white sauce
1 gallon pop corn (hot buttered)

Serve white sauce into individual bowls and serve a tablespoon of popped corn into each bowl.

Utah State Agricultural College
Extension Service
1935 (#NS 80)

Dishwasher

This is possibly a machine of the future. A few different kinds are on the market, but for the small family at home they seem not yet entirely successful. The Home Economics Department of the Utah Agricultural College is experimenting now, with more or less practical results, on small machines advertised as being adapted to the use of the ordinary family.

Certainly nothing is more needed in all the homes of the civilized world than some satisfactory solution of the "dish washing problem."

Utah Agricultural College Experiment Station
Extension Division
1912 (#6 [7?])

FOOTBALL PRACTICE

They had funds in the athletic department. We finally came around with good equipment, as good as they had. After the first two weeks of football, then we'd take off for two weeks harvest vacation. The whole school, all the schools let out, and for two weeks they were out in the beet and potato fields. And our football players were throwing potatoes instead of footballs. The work in the fields kept them in shape, but you don't get any football practice hugging a potato.

Heber Whiting

DARK OF THE MOON

Never plant your potatoes in the light of the moon. They'll be all tops.

Wait until the last dark of the moon in the month of May before you plant potatoes. That way no frost will ruin the crops.

Hog butchering should be carried out during the dark of the moon. If butchering is done while the moon is increasing, the bacon will bubble up and increase and not fry out.

A woman scrubs potatoes outdoors in a wash tub. (Special Collections and Archives. Utah State University.)

POTATO PAY

We'd go and dig potatoes for either a bushel or a bushel and a half a day or something like that. All the work was done for what we could get back in edibles. You know, potatoes—something that we didn't raise—we could take our pay in potatoes or take it in money.

Fred Kuhni
Heber City

BEST CROP

When you summer fallow, all that rain goes right into the ground, and the snow comes along and covers it up, and there's lots of moisture there the next year. And then we don't have to depend entirely on rain, but as a rule, got enough rain—just when we needed it. I had these potatoes—they were all sprouted—and I thought, well, when I was going to throw them away, "I'll just go plant them in this back furrow." So I got in the truck and went about half a mile, and I planted them in this back furrow. It was June, the first of June, so I didn't expect I'd get anything. But that was the best crop of potatoes I ever had. And I always raised a good garden out there. We'd only have to water it about once. We'd water the potatoes once and the peas once, and the rest of it along with the peas, and that was about all it needed, because we'd always pick a spot where it was kind of level and the snow'd lay late.

Phebe Smith
Randolph

Farming Experience

I'll say [farming] was a great experience! Everything is up to you then. You either make it or not. Nothing gets done unless you go do it yourself. That was the worst thing in my life that I had to do was to quit the farm. Everywhere you looked there was work to do all the time, and you come down here on a city lot, and I don't know how I ever stood it. I would even get up in the night going out to see what I could do. It's worse than going on a mission and coming home and getting relocated again. We lived there fifty-five years. I had 840 acres. You feel like you're part of everything when you plow it and put in and see it go in and watch it grow and watch it mature and then you cut it and put it in a bin and then take it to market. It just makes you feel like you're a part of it.

Pierce Hardman
North Logan

Wash Day Beans

From the store we got dry beans. We'd have a variety of beans, about a half a dozen different kinds of beans, and so we never got tired of those. Larry, I had to laugh at him because he'd say to me after I had my own children, I'd always cook the beans on wash day. Because I didn't have time to do all this frying and stuff. I'd put them to soak the night before, you know, and then I'd get up and put those on to cook and then start to wash.

Eva Campbell Bybee
Providence

"Green beans are one of the main crops of the area." Cache County, August 1940. (Photo by Russell Lee for Farm Security Administration, Library of Congress.)

MIDWIFE'S FEE

Our doctor was at Randolph. I might mention that when I came to town, the old midwife was Sister Wahlstrom, and her fee was $5. Sometimes she would take it out in spuds if you didn't have the cash, or she would take it out in vegetables. She didn't only be there at the delivery of the child. She was there to help out for two weeks, ten days after.

Ray Lamborn

TONS OF TOMATOES

Arthur Firth, I rented ground from him, and one year I had twelve acres of tomatoes in. I had an old account book around here where I delivered 800 tons of tomatoes to these three factories.

Harry Lunn
Ogden

MUSHROOM CROP

Eggs would bring about 15¢ a dozen. Radishes and onions, a nice bunch about like that, tied and trimmed up would bring anywhere from five to ten cents. Onions.

There was a pueblo that had been built out there on this place I rented from that little Swedish woman — 113 acres. When I became twenty-one I rented that. This old pueblo had been of mud and bullrushes and all that stuff, and it caved in and just made a mound. You've heard of the mounds all up through the country here. What it is is them old pueblos. They left a mound when they melted down.

I noticed in the spring that'd steam, and there was no snow lay on it, so I went and took the old plow, and I started around. Just kept plowing around and around. And then I went to a seed store, and I bought all the sweepings from back of the counter. So it had everything in it, and I broadcasted that [on the mound]. I got eight dollars of garden stuff off that mound. And mushrooms. I had to pay [the Swedish lady] extra for the mushrooms. We made so much money on them that she charged me extra on the rent, but we'd get 40¢ a pound for them. One time Mother, Will, and I went and, and we got us a hundred pounds—$40 worth. And Will needed a suit of clothes. A suit of clothes only cost him $18, so we made pretty good that morning.

Harry Lunn
Ogden

JAPANESE BEET WORKERS

When we thinned beets, Father took the metal off of the wagon box, cut it in so many pieces, doubled it over, hammered it down, got it loose, and turned it over one end over. He sharpened that. Then we had to take rugs, and we bound the yarn clear up about six or seven inches long and made the handle. And I said they were horrible. I told him that. I said, "They're horrible, Father." But we had to thin the beets, you know, with pads on our knees. We wore long stockings and petticoats crawling up those

49 ॐ

"Providence First Ward sauerkraut experts" created a tasty
product that gave rise to the tradition of church-sponsored
turkey and sauerkraut fund-raising dinners, c. 1950.
(Providence and Her People, Watkins Printing Co., 1974.)

50

beet rows. After a while we got so that we could stoop over and pull the weeds and do that. We had a pretty good crop of beets. Then we'd help top them and get them to the factory on the wagon box. The Japs came in then, and one of them came and asked him if they could have a job. He had Father tie a bunch of sacks under him. They went around doing people's beets. So they let him live in the creamery over from his house up in the top. They went through those beet patches like lightning. They would just stoop over, and away they would go. Father said, "Those fools are going to ruin all those beets." But they didn't. We had a good crop of beets. I was sure glad that that man took it over.

Annie Leishman
Wellsville

Summer Income

I used to work all summer for a neighbor thinning beets. My neighbor used to give me a little more for thinning beets because I did it well, and that made me proud. [We got] about 8¢ a row. I got 9¢, and we'd try to make a dollar a day.

Heber Whiting

Cabbage Furrow

My father used to raise his garden, and he'd raise cabbage. And then in the fall of the year when he'd raise cabbage, he'd plow a furrow, and they'd put some straw in that furrow. And then he'd put the cabbage upside head down, roots sticking up. And they'd put straw and dirt over the top of those cabbage, and they'd lay there, and they'd keep til spring. Then when you wanted cabbage, you'd go out and pull on the end of it and pull one out.

Harvey Merrill
Hyrum

GRASSHOPPERS

in the Spring of 1868 the wether got warm And all Crops was in then the Grassopers began to opp around and the ground was black with them And in A few weeks they was taking all every thing And we was trying every way to Kill or do away with them we dugg trenches in our wheat two and three feet deep And then would drive them in And we Catched a great maney that way And Some would drive them into the Creeks And Catch them that way but as a rule they took all the grain which made us go off to work in the Railroad and roads from the East And west was Coming into Utah grain was worth 5 dollers per bushel but we had none Potatoes was worth 150 and 2 dollers a bushel but we made good Money on the Rail Roads in the winter I made four trips out to the Promentery with Lumber and Potatoes and did pretty well

Charles Ramsden Bailey

For coldsores, eat a lot of cabbage.

CANNING VS. STORAGE

To can vegetables which can be stored is a waste of bottles and energy. It is often desirable to have a few bottles of vegetables on hand for cases of emergency. The canning of such is best done when some of the bottles are being emptied in the late fall when the heat has subsided and the housewife's rush of summer work is over.

Utah Agricultural College
Extension Division
1917 (#25)

BACTERIA

Since canning is a means of preserving food from bacteria, it is well to know something of their characteristics. First, they are so small that they are invisible except under a powerful lense. On this account people either don't believe in them or forget about them.

Second, the air, the dust, and all objects are covered with them.

Third, temperature affects them. Cold, even to freezing point, does not kill them, but only prevents their growth. Sunshine and scalding heat, applied a certain length of time, destroys them. Moderate heat or normal body temperature is the best possible medium for their growth.

Utah Agricultural College
Extension Division
1917 (#18)

"Wife of a Mormon farmer with canned goods." Snowville,
August 1940. (Photo by Russell Lee for Farm Security
Administration, Library of Congress.)

CANNED BAKED POTATOES

These may be canned by mashing dry and packing into jars. Seal jars tightly and sterilize in wash boiler 40 minutes, pressure cooker 10 minutes under 10 pounds pressure. Remove jars and wrap in paper.

Utah Agricultural College
Extension Division
1917 (#18)

EXAMINATION OF CANNED PRODUCTS BEFORE TASTING OR SERVING

1. Jars should be free from leaks. Tin cans should have both ends slightly curved inward. Neither end should bulge or snap back when pressed. Seams should be tight and free from leaks.

2. When opened, the odor should be characteristic of the fresh product. Any different odor, color, or texture probably denotes spoilage.

3. DO NOT TASTE MEAT OR VEGETABLES UNTIL THEY HAVE BEEN BOILED 10 MINUTES. Observe odor after boiling.

4. Examine inside of can to see that it is free from corrosion. Protein products will darken an unenameled can, but this should not be mistaken for corrosion.

5. Any canned food which shows signs of spoilage either by odor or appearance should be BURNED or destroyed with strong lye.

"Sweet corn and the daughter of a Mormon farmer." Snowville, August 1940. (Photo by Russell Lee for Farm Security Administration, Library of Congress.)

6. Spoiled foods should not be fed to animals even after products have been boiled, nor should they be buried. Botulinus bacteria thrive in the soil.

Utah Agricultural College
Extension Service
1934 (#NS 63)

BILLS TO PAY

Well, our light bill would be about $1 a month, and our taxes wouldn't be over $35 a year on the house. This included taxes on our farm and everything. And that was about all we really needed money for, unless we had some emergencies.

However, we always had some cash crops that came in the fall of the year. We always had some sugar beets, and then we would get these sugar beet checks. When this would happen, Dad would go up and buy all our clothes, shoes and everything we needed to get us ready for winter. So when winter came along, it didn't take very much money to get us through.

Joseph Christian Jacobsen
Logan

WORLD WAR I

Well, I wanted to join the Army, but I wasn't eighteen yet, and my mother put her arms around me and said, "Son, the day you turn eighteen you can join." And I think she was smart. My birthday was on the 21st of November, but the war ended on the 11th.

[The effect of the war] was tremendous. You can't imagine all the men who went. . . . It took all the men out. In fact, I was sixteen and seventeen at the time, and two of us kids that age did all the farm work, pitching hay. I remember during the war our wages went up, and we got $5 a day in that last summer. That was unheard of. We used to work for a dollar and a half, $2 a day. We worked hard for it, and we were proud of it. In fact, my step-father told my brother and I that if we'd plant and take care of his twenty acres of beets, we could have half of it. Well, you never saw beets so beautiful in all your life. We averaged twenty-two tons to the acre, and we got $12 a ton.

Heber Whiting

World War II

We changed our crops because at the time of the war it was so hard to get help. We were still raising beets during the war, and at that time they had the war prisoners down where the fairgrounds are. They would have these prisoners go out under guard and have them help the farmers harvest their crops. At that time Floyd was married and living in the house where Morgans live now. He had beets down there, and we had beets, and the prisoners would come out. All they would have for their lunch — I felt so bad about it — it looked like just a slice of bread or something. It was not very appetizing. We felt sorry for them because they worked so hard. Zenath and I, Floyd's first wife, would fix dinner and take down to them while they were working. They would have the guards there with their guns watching them to see that nobody escaped. When we took those dinners down to them, they were so appreciative. Very, very appreciative.

Eva Mae Israelson
North Logan

Work Clothes

Well, my two younger sisters, Edna and Elsie, wore coveralls or overalls and shirts when working in the fields, but my older sister and I wore short-sleeved dresses made of cotton materials. We made sleeves to protect our arms from the sun by cutting the toes out of long cotton stockings, making a hole for the thumb, and pinning the top of the stocking to our short sleeves. We wore big straw hats to protect our faces from the sun. We had white canvas gloves to wear when we used the shovel or sugar beet knife on a cold, frosty morning.

Beth Wyatt Winn
Salt Lake City

Fourth of July Peas

They had a big grove of trees up there, a grove of poplar trees, and every holiday in the summer and the spring they would have a big picnic up there. Mrs. Warner was the hostess always of those picnics. I remember on the Fourth of July she always had a big kettle of green

Utah State University harvest queen candidates pose for a publicity photo, c. 1945–50. (Special Collections and Archives. Utah State University.)

peas and new potatoes, and I can just remember how they tasted. They were really good, and she was a real hostess. She was just a charming woman. She had the sweetest smile, and everybody loved her.

Lydia Ann Taylor Skewes
Moab

Diary, 1850

Saturday 11 I ploughed and harrowed and furrowed out a piece of land for corn
Sunday 12 I staid at home and coppied Sister Walkers blessing
Monday 13 I ploughed
Tuesday 14 the same
Wednesday 15 I harrowed the land I ploughed the 2 days before
Thursday 16 I ploughed my potatoes
Friday 17 I planted my melons
Saturday 18 I planted pompions squashes and corn
Sunday 19 this day I am at home as Agnes is sick of the meazles and had been for two days

John Borrowman

Cellar Storage

We did have an excavation under the kitchen floor on that addition on the north. They took buckets and dug out down as far as the potrock would let them. They just used

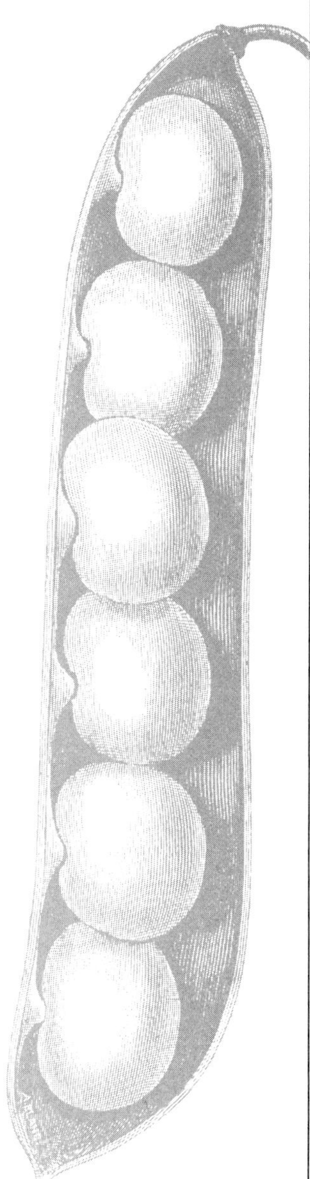

61 ❧

it for storage. We used it for a potato pit. We'd carry them in buckets or sacks and dump them down there, and we'd sort them and rick them around. It was ideal because it was right under the house, nice and cool. And carrots, turnips, and stuff like that that would keep was stored under that floor. Sometimes it'd be so full you could barely get down to pick up a turnip there and potato there and carrot over here.

Fred Kuhni
Heber City

Pit Storage

It seems like everyone had a garden. We couldn't have survived without a garden. We had parsnips we'd put away for the winter. They'd have parsnips still out in the ground and go out in the spring and get them out. They put straw over them to protect them. They dug holes in the ground for potatoes and apples, too, and put them in what we called pits. They put about a foot of straw over the top and covered it over with dirt. And they'd be just as crisp and nice when you'd dig in there in the spring. . . .

Mother, one year, just put them in milk cans. Put carrots in milk cans and put the lids on, and they kept beautifully. We had put them in tubs in sand, but this one year she did it with milk cans, and they were just as crisp.

Lloyd and Arlynn Olsen
Paradise

"Mrs. Christiansen of the Christiansen canning unit sealing cans. During 1939 she canned 2,300 quarts which included 20 sheep, 2 deer, 2 beeves, 5 pigs. Fish was tried very successfully. In this cooperative agreement there are 25 users, and outside the cooperative there are 10 others who used Mrs. Christiansen's services." Box Elder County, September 1940. (Photo by Russell Lee for Farm Security Administration, Library of Congress.)

Pickles

Well, one time they decided they wanted some pickles, and the boss hadn't furnished any pickles. So I bought a keg of pickles, and that's when we was camped down on the Duchesne. The two [sheep] herds were down between Wolf Creek and Box Canyon that year, and I was coming down the mountain. I was coming down what they call Trail Canyon, and then the trail went right down the face of the mountain to the river. And that keg of pickles worked loose. I had it between the trees of the pack saddle. I thought it was lashed on, and it just went down that mountain like a big rock. And at the bottom there was this big old tree that'd been killed by fire, and it hit that, and it just sent pickles both ways. I was able to gather up just a handful. I found maybe a dozen pickles down in the brush out of that old keg.

Harry Lunn
Ogden

Beefsteak Spinach

Take one jar of green olives and eat the olives as usual. Simmer spinach in the olive juice. It tastes as good as beefsteak. People just go back for more.

Walt Lichfield
Providence

Dill Pickles

Pack dill size cukes in sterile jars
2 large sprays of dill for each 2 qt. jar
Add ⅓ T. powdered alum and cover with brine boiling hot.
4 qts. water
2 cups vinegar
1 cup salt
Cap with old fashioned Mason lids

Dedicated to Robert who loved these pickles.

Eulalia Welch Sorensen
Mendon

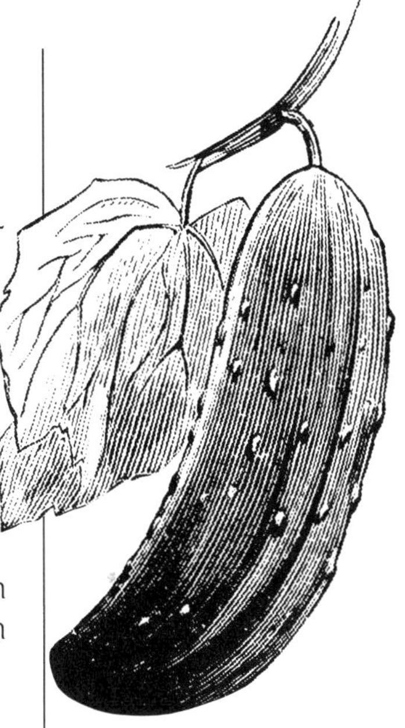

Tithing 1876

Oats 160 lbs
Wheat 780 lbs
Squash 810 lbs
Potatoes 674 lbs

John Fitzgerald
Draper

If you peel a cucumber from the top toward the root, it will not be bitter. But if it is peeled from the root up, it will be bitter.

Yellow Squash

We used to raise these little thin squashes. They were little tiny round yellow squash. They were real good. My mother used to cook them every day. Well, besides pota-

toes and gravy. We always had potatoes and gravy — and
then these little squash. She'd put on a kettle of potatoes
to boil, and then she'd have a little kind of colander thing.
And then she'd put it full of these little squash and then
put it on top of the potatoes. And they'd steam done from
the steam from the potatoes, and they were really good.
I haven't seen any of those for years. I guess they just don't
have them anymore. I've tasted some that taste something
like it, but nothing can equal those little thin squash that
we used to have.

Lydia Ann Taylor Skewes
Moab

Patriotic Duty

It is the patriotic duty of every American citizen to help
in every way possible in the production and conservation
of our food products. One of the very best ways of doing
this is to economize in food waste. To waste anything is
a crime. Women and girls can help in this important matter by canning and putting up for next winter fruits, vegetables, meats, soups, anything and everything that will have
a food value. The high cost of living, the shortage of food
supplies, have made it necessary to urge this matter very
earnestly.

Utah Agricultural College
Extension Division
1917 (#18)

Workers in this cannery scene may be Mormon volunteers contributing their labors to the church relief program, c. 1940. (Special Collections and Archives. Utah State University.)

Woods Cross Cannery

In West Bountiful we used to use many of the boys and the kids in the area to weed the onions and cut the asparagus in the spring of the year, which was taken over to the Woods Cross Cannery, where the Phillips 66 building is now. That was part of the old Woods Cross Cannery. We used to go over there in the fall and work putting up tomatoes. Many of the girls in the area worked at the Woods Cross Cannery. That's where they got their money to go to school and buy their clothes in the fall and for the winter. Summer work was done by piece work, and others was done by the hour. Most of it run about all the way from 25¢ an hour to about 35¢ an hour is what we used to get paid at the cannery.

Lester Knighton
Bountiful

Cooking Greens

The first step in making greens acceptable to the family palate is wise selection, using at first those mild in flavor, such as pigweed, lamb's quarters, and milkweed; later, the stronger flavored ones may be acceptable.

The second and highly important step is to wash the greens entirely free from grit. This precaution often makes the difference between an enjoyment of greens and a dislike for them.

Utah State Agricultural College
Utah Experiment Station
1934 (#104)

MIDWIFE

My mother didn't like that too much as a midwife. We'd go to bed at night, and we didn't know whether we'd have somebody to cook our breakfast next morning or not, because we figured if some newcomer came to town, my mother would be called out.

Ray Lamborn

GROCERIES

Everything was by the case and the sack. In fact, if we hadn't bought in the fall, we began to have to buy two. We had a long winter ahead of us. Buy two cases, buy two or three sacks of stuff. I never did buy one can. I see people go in there and buy one can, and I say, "Good laws, that wouldn't last only one meal." And I am still buying stuff by the case. I never got out of the habit.

Pierce Hardman
North Logan

SHARING

Well, we were in an earlier culture where hay and grain and a few potatoes was enough to feed us. We never thought of growing enough potatoes to sell to anyone else. If we had extra potatoes, some of the neighbors might be short, and we tried to see to it that they got what they

A largely Indian crew poses to have a picture taken during a day of potato planting. (Compton Collection. Special Collections and Archives. Utah State University.)

needed. Potatoes weren't a commodity to be sold or bartered. It was something to be given to your neighbors if they needed it.

Burton Tew
St. George

GARDEN TITHE

Yes, [they tithed] for every bit of stuff they reaped out of the garden. If she dug her carrots in the fall, whatever they took out in carrots, ten percent of it was given to the church. And the same with the potatoes. When they dug potatoes, every tenth bushel went to the church. Through the eggs, every tenth dozen went to the church for tithing. Very, very precise in their tithing.

Fred Kuhni
Heber City

SECOND-FAMILY FARM

Mother and him were married, well I don't remember just what time. But they had the children, see, and soon after, well five years after they were in Laketown, my uncle William was married. He died. I believe it was appendicitis that was the cause of his death. He left his widow, Eunice, with two small girls. Now at the time they were practicing polygamy, and my father and my mother prayed about it, and it tells you in the Bible if your brother dies, you should take his wife and raise his family. So they decided just themselves that he would marry my aunt Eunice, his brother's wife. Through this union they had five boys and one girl, and as long as I was in Laketown we always worked together on the farm. I can remember my father, as I was a boy growing up, he would work a half day for us and a half day for the other family. Now the other family, or Aunt Eunice, lived on the property where Norma Lee and Dean live at this present time. We had the property in the north field and in the west field. You could raise potatoes in the north field where you couldn't out in this south field, so they always had a batch of potatoes alongside of ours. My father would let them have the ground, see. We had the same equipment, and we planted potatoes, and we worked together. That's the way we grew up, all up until the time I left Laketown. We were working together as brothers. I worked with Dick and Bill. We had the same equipment. We bought the mower and rakes together. We didn't have enough property to have machinery for each one. We worked together, and there was no trouble at all. We grew up as brothers.

Ray Lamborn

DANDELIONS

My father—I don't know his education, but he was everybody's friend and adviser. . . . He was a good fellow. I always kind of thought I was his pet. Twice a year we'd go up to the grist mill to have our wheat ground. I'll always remember the spring when all the dandelions were out. And he'd let me out, and I'd go pick the dandelions and bring them home. We'd come home with fifty pounds

The Jensen Brothers Milling and Elevator Company shows off its product in a parade float, c. 1908. (Compton Collection. Special Collections and Archives. Utah State University.)

of wheat and 100 pounds of dandelions. He was patient with me, and I loved him, and I was sorry to lose him. He had a wonderful sense of humor.

Heber Whiting

NEW MILLER

Well, I came from England from my mission, and I was asked by my father if I would go and take over the Central Milling Company in Laketown which he had purchased while I was on my mission. I told my dad that I didn't know a thing about flour milling. "Well," he says, "you're a pretty smart fellow, and you could learn." So I went up. I told my dad that I didn't know any more about flour milling than a pig knows about Sunday, but I took over this flour mill.

Herbert R. Weston
Logan

BREAD MAKER

Mother made eight loaves of bread every other day. She could break off the dough and shape them in her hand. She never laid them on a board. I tried, and I can't do it.

Arlynn Olsen
Paradise

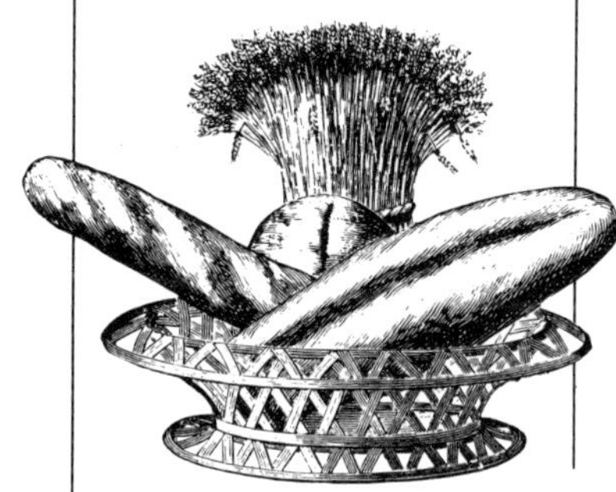

Granary

The only granary we ever had on that place is the one I wrote about in my diary. When Dad bought the place he bought this log cabin. The log cabin, I would say, was not bigger than ten by twelve—maybe ten by fourteen. Dad and Mother lived in that log cabin for a short period of time—until in the summer when Dad harvested his grain and he had no place to put the grain except in a part of the log cabin. So he split this log cabin the first year or two, until he would build a two room house.

Burton Tew
St. George

Relief Society

Well, the Relief Society used to go around and gather up whatever a farmer had—wheat and such as that—and store it in this granary they had here in Cove. Then they'd make it into flour and give it to the poor people, people that really needed it. Just the very poor people. There was no relief, what they called relief, at that time. When they paid their tithing here in this ward, they used to have what they called a tithing office yard over here. They'd turn a cow in, a steer, or anything, you know. A load of hay. That was the way a lot of them paid their tithing that way. It was collected because they had no money.

Ambrious Larsen
Cove

Men, women, and children work together to gather in the
grain harvest in 1896. (Special Collections and Archives. Utah
State University.)

CRICKETS, 1849

In plowing the land, we selected damp land around willows and spring holes and much of it proved to be mineral where crops would not grow. Then the crickets came down off the mountains apparently on purpose to destroy our crops that were growing. We made small wooden paddles and with these we all turned out for over one month and worked as hard to fight crickets as in a field of battle. By our faithful struggle and the aid of the seagulls that came to our aid there was a portion of our crops saved. When harvest time came my father took sick and having no reapers or cradles my oldest sister, Caroline, and myself took each a butcher knife to harvest what wheat there was left after the crickets had done their work. When we had threshed the wheat with flails we had 20 bushels. The corn, beans, and other graden truck was destroyed by the crickets.

Goudy E. Hogan

GRASSHOPPERS, 1871

I plowed and sowed as usual hoping every year would be the last year that the hoppers would come to visit us. This year I sowed more grain than the year before and felt determined to struggle and try again this season to head off the grasshoppers by making a water ditch over half mile long above my farm. I dug the ditch so that the grasshoppers could not so easily catch hold as they would be floating downstream and carried into Cub River. The grasshoppers did destroy nearly all the crops around above me

and when they had destroyed nearly all the crops around me they descended on mine. But they fell in the water ditch and floated away. Some were able to catch on and climb up the side. To stop this myself and entire family and some others struggled and fought them down, burning straw next to the bank working sabbath day and all and finally saved the crops. Bishop Merrill remarked that I made more water ditches than all Richmond together. This was the first good crop that I have raised for seven years. I was very thankful to the Lord that he had given me wisdom to head off the destroyers once for I stood in great need of a crop to help me out of debt. I felt that I was a free man once more that is I was not altogether out of debt but the prospects were good if the hoppers would leave our lands. Once more I raised over 700 bushels of grains while many lost all their crops.

Goudy E. Hogan

War Wheat Substitutes

The wheat substitutes are: bran, shorts, middlings, corn flour, cornmeal, edible cornstarch, hominy, corn grits, barley flour, rolled oats, oatmeal, rice, rice flour, buckwheat flour, potato flour, sweet potato flour, milo flours and similar flours and meals, bean meal, peanut meal, casava, taro, and banana flours, and other products of a similar nature.

Rye was a substitute until March 31 when it was withdrawn from the substitute list because a shortage of rye flour was threatened.

Utah Agricultural College
Extension Division
1918 (#21)

*"Daughter of a Mormon farmer, sweeping up the kitchen."
Snowville, August 1940. (Photo by Russell Lee for Farm Security
Administration, Library of Congress.)*

Wood Stove

Yes, I had to chop wood. The first three years after I was married all I used to see was that axe, and I chopped wood. We kept [the fire] going at night. Every morning we had to thaw out everything. Everything would be froze. Then we had to thaw it out before you could get breakfast. I don't know how we got through them winters.

Pierce Hardman
North Logan

Navajo Fry Bread

3 cups flour
1 tablespoon baking powder
½ teaspoon salt
¼ cup powdered milk
1½ cups warm water
Lard or other shortening

Combine ingredients in a large bowl. Add the warm water in small amounts and knead dough until soft but not sticky. Cover and let stand about 15 minutes.

Pull off large egg-sized balls of dough and roll into rounds about ¼ inch thick. Punch a hole in the center of each round, to allow dough to puff. Fry in lard or shortening in a heavy skillet.

Serve with powdered sugar or jam or with salt.

A whole dinner's menu might be mutton stew, fry bread, and coffee.

Miiko Toelken
Logan

Tortillas

    2 cups flour
    2 teaspoons baking powder
    1 teaspoon salt
    2 tablespoons melted lard
    Enough water to make a dough that can be rolled out

Cover and let stand for at least an hour. Form in small ball, pat or roll out. Grease a grill with lard and heat to medium heat. Cook tortillas on grill.

For enchiladas, use less baking powder and double the amount of shortening and roll very thin.

Ernestine learned how to make tortillas from her mother, Lugarda Suazo.

Ernestine Gonzoles
Ephriam

Burt Martin's Movie Show

Before then we'd call Burt Martin's show. We used to get megaphones and go around the town hollering, "Burt Martin's show tonight! Cowboys and Indians!" Then there'd be some that go uptown and some go lower town, and as we'd go, we'd go clear to lower town and then come back. We always used to stop at these Greek places where they had Greek boarding houses. Go in there, we'd always get a piece of Greek bread. That old French bread, like French. They used to give us candy and bread and cheese, Greek cheese. We'd always go in to call on them. Then we'd go out hollering, "Burt Martin's show!"

Howard T. Jones
Sunnyside

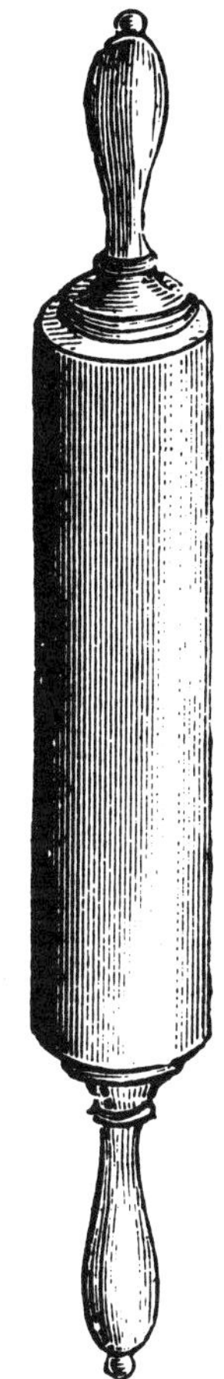

A threshing crew works near American Fork, c. 1890–1900.
(Special Collections and Archives. Utah State University.)

Helping With the Threshing

Another exciting time would be when it was time for the threshing of the wheat to take place. We used to follow the threshing machine, and it was a steam engine. Mark Painter was the operator, and when they would come to your home, we would have to feed them. As kids we would get up on the back of the old steam engine and blow the whistle when it was time to eat. We would get in the grain bins and push the grain around in our bare feet so they could make room for more. And it really was quite an experience to follow the threshing machine and watch how it worked.

Joseph Christian Jacobsen
Logan

Threshing Meals

They would used to tell about some of the [threshing] outfits that would get to some place where the woman was a right good cook, why, they would kind of stall so that they would be there for supper and breakfast the next morning so that they would get a couple of extra good meals out of it.

Vaughn Scott

THRESHERS

One of my best girlfriends lived a mile north of us, LaRue Leishman. Her father was James "Jim" Leishman. We'd walk back and forth helping one another with work. Especially did we enjoy the days when the threshers were eating at either house!

Beth Wyatt Winn
Salt Lake City

FEEDING THE THRESHERS

We did have some threshing. One day Mother and my sister went to the G.A.R. program in Salt Lake, the parade and all. The Grand Army of the Republic. After she was gone we heard we were going to have threshers the next day. She and my big sister was gone, so I got busy and prepared for the threshers. Me and my brother was there. Hazelton. . . . I went to pick beans and got a big kettle of string beans. And potatoes. Mother always had, oh, ham or something like that to make some gravy. I would say that we had turnips, too. I liked turnips. All of us liked turnips. And so I'd fix them for a second vegetable. And then we had fruit. The peaches weren't ripe yet, but we had apricots and tomatoes. Mother always bottled it in two-quart bottles, so we had plenty of that.

Eva Campbell Bybee
Providence

QUANTITIES OF WATER AND COOKING TIME OF CEREALS

Cereal — 1 cup	*Water*	*Time*
Finely ground as Cream of Wheat, Germade, etc.	4 cups	1 hour
Coarse or flaked as Roman meal or Rolled Oats	2½ to 3 cups	1 to 2 hours
Whole or coarsely cracked cereals	6 to 8 cups	4 to 8 hours

Utah State Agricultural College
Extension Service
1930 (#NS 24)

PARCHED WHEAT

Wheat can be soaked or cooked until tender and then fried or deep fried until brown and crunchy. You can use parched wheat like nuts with raisins in divinity. It can also be flavored with salt and pepper or seasoning salts of various kinds.

Genevieve Bundy
Dixie

A four-horse team is used to harvest potatoes on the Sevier Experimental Farm in October 1919. (Special Collections and Archives. Utah State University.)

PANOLIE

Grind dried corn quite fine. Brown in frying pan, stirring constantly. Do NOT use oil. Serve cold with cream and sugar if desired.

Genevieve Bundy
Dixie

COAL STOVE BREAD

I used to sit with my feet on the oven door with a good magazine and an apple to eat. Oh, it was fun. Bread baked out of a coal stove was delicious.

Arlynn Olsen
Paradise

BREAD AND DUCK

Do you know how to make Bread and Duck? I'd sit down to the table, and my mother used to set a big glass of milk in front of me. I'd take a piece of bread and duck it in there and then eat it.

Harvey Merrill
Hyrum

DRY FARMING LIFE

[Your] wife's the other half. I had a good woman. Never heard her say [if she liked living on the dry farm.] She just said, "As long as you're around, I don't care."

Pierce Hardman
North Logan

Dry Farming Equipment

Apart from the necessary buildings and fence, the following ought to be provided to meet economical ends, under ordinary conditions.

Approximate
Cost, 1917

4 or 5 Horses 1300 lbs. to 1400 lbs. (2 or 3 can be mares)	$750.00
1 Farm Wagon 3¼	140.00
1 Set Farm Harnesses	65.00
3 Single Harnesses for Plow	60.00
1 Set Railroad Rails for Grubbing	25.00
1 Gang Plow	85.00
2 Sections "Nephi" Harrow	45.00
1 Sixteen Drop Grain Drill	150.00
⅓ Interest in 12 foot Header	90.00
1 Header Box	35.00

$1445.00

Agricultural College of Utah
Extension Division
1920 (#2)

Biscuits! Biscuits!

[Mother] says that crossing the plains they would find a buffalo which they killed, and that was the meat that they'd have to eat. Of course, she came over with the hand-cart company. One night she was awakened and she could

A home economics student practices her bread baking skills.
C. 1905. (Special Collections and Archives. Utah State University.)

hear people calling, "Biscuits! Biscuits!" It was a relief party that Brigham Young had sent to meet them because he knew that they were out of food and their shoes were worn out from crossing the plains.

Iris Kunz Buhler
Midvale

SCONES

Utah scones are not related to the dense, baked British variety, but are a light, kneaded dough deep fried. They are most commonly served with honey butter—a blend of two of the state's other specialties.

  2 cups scalded milk
  ¾ cup sugar
  1 tablespoon salt
  3 eggs, beaten
  ⅔ cup shortening or oil
  3 tablespoons yeast

Add enough flour to make easy kneading—about 12 cups. Knead dough until smooth and soft. Put in greased bowl and allow to rise until double in bulk. Continue to punch down until ready to fry the scones in deep fat. Pat or roll into circles about 6 inches in diameter and fry.

Lynn and Janice Sanders
Hurricane

Threshing Crew Cook

[My grandmother] cooked for a threshing crew when she was thirteen years old. I remember her saying she started at 3:00 in the morning, started her bread. She'd make fresh bread every day for the threshing crew. I can't remember how many loaves she said she made every day. Something like twelve or thirteen loaves a day.

Alan Godfrey
Garland

Recipe for Biscuit

From one who has made biscuit for her husband for forty-three years and he is still alive and in the best of health.

To 1 pint of flour 2 Hp tsp. B Powd
1 teaspoon full of Salt Sift all together
Then work in 1 Hp Tab.spoon of Snowdrift
More or less to suit yourself
Then add ½ pint of milk or water
Cook quickly in a hot oven but not hot enough to burn

Mrs. Etta C. Ellis

From the recipe file of
Eulalia Welch Sorensen
Mendon

Thanksgiving Rolls

My favorite thing my mom made is fresh rolls, hot rolls. At Thanksgiving dinner I'm always the last one eating, sitting there finishing up the rolls.

Gordon Andrus
Logan

Gypsies

Then another thing that worried me was the gypsies. We had gypsies, and they were what we really walked in dread of. If you look at the television now when there is gypsies on it, they're just duplicates of what we had then. They camped up the road in wagon loads, and they would come every day to the place for things. There was the two families there—Frank Wyatt and John Wyatt—and we were told to give them some milk. This one girl would come down, and she would say, "My, you drink a lot of milk."

I asked Mother if I could give her just a gallon can of milk twice a day because that was our living, to get our milk check from the dairy. Anyway, she says, "Give them the milk. If you don't, they'll steal it." So one day, one of them come in with beads all on, earrings and everything, and so she said, "I've got a little teensy weensy baby up there that needs some milk." I said, "That little baby must drink a lot of milk." But I was nice to her, and I filled her bucket up and let her go.

Annie Leishman
Wellsville

Dairy cows pastured in Manti National Forest are milked.
C. 1925–35. (Special Collections and Archives. Utah State
University.)

PRANKS

Well, we went over to Angus Bowman's place, and we took his horses out and put them over in Henry Firth's cow barn, and Firth's cows in Gus Bowman's stables. Henry always had his wife go along and hold the lantern for him when he went out to milk the cows. They went out there in the stable. His wife told us on him after. He says, "Give me that lantern." He looked at the animals. Then he said, "These are not cows. These are horses."

Harry Lunn
Ogden

FIRST AUTOMOBILE

I remember well the first automobile that went through Woodruff. I remember how most of the horses in town run away, those that were on the street. The one that happened to be running the milk wagon, I remember, for Father, the team run away and run into a tree, spilled all the milk, and caused quite a bit of excitement.

J. Earl Stuart
Randolph

FRESH MILK

We churned our own butter and skimmed off the cream off the top. Many, many times the cats'd be following us around while we milked the cows and get a squirt of fresh milk from the udder. It was fun. I'm glad we've got some of the things we've got today, but the old times—.

Shirley M. Griffin
Brigham City

Dog Power

This milk operation that they had up there, they used to churn butter there. And they had a dog that used to tread a waterwheel that used to churn the butter for them. They didn't have to do the work themselves. They had this old hound dog do it for them.

Lester Knighton
Bountiful

Grocery Bill

Well, [people] went on relief or they had this Hoover project, road project, that they could go on. But I had a few chickens, a few sheep, a trap line. So we got along. We raised our own food, a good deal of it—what we had to eat, anyway. So the only thing we'd have to buy was our clothing and our sugar and a few groceries that we bought. I mentioned, oh, just this week we went to the grocery store, and we bought stuff that came to just under a hundred dollars—a few canned goods, a few things like that that you can bring home in the back seat of an automobile. Our grocery bill at Laketown used to be around

A small child helps churn butter with a handmade pottery churn, c. 1912. (Special Collections and Archives. Utah State University.)

two hundred dollars a year. We'd pay it. We would usually run a bill there, and when we would shear the sheep or sell the lambs or we had some fur money, we'd go pay our store bill.

Ray Lamborn

CHURNING

Churning milk? Oh yes. We used to shake it in a bottle, a two-quart bottle, to get our butter. Then Mother got one of these old churns that churns it with the wood paddle in the bottom. It was a lot easier than shaking the bottle.

Reginald Rawlins
Cove

BUTTER FOR CORINNE

My father gathered eggs and butter from the country north of here, and he hauled them to Corinne with an ox team. He had to travel over the mountain west of here, north of the Bear River Canyon, because there was no bridge over the Bear River between here and Cache Junction. He traveled back and forth with his eggs and butter to Corinne, Utah.

Jessie Barker
Newton

Finishing the Butter

Carefully mould the butter into neat one-pound prints and wrap it in strong parchment paper made for this purpose. Make the prints as attractive as possible and handle carefully when packing. Keep the butter in a cool place and sell it while fresh. Aim to make the best butter in the State.

Experiment Station of the Agricultural College of Utah
1906 (#96)

Canyon Summer

I had a mother and a dad that loved to go in the canyons. And I had an uncle Thomas Osgethorpe that owned a cabin right at the head of East Millcreek Canyon, and we used to go up there every summer and spend two weeks. We'd go up in a wagon and a horse, take our cow and tie it to the back of it—the wagon. And we'd go for two weeks. We took the cow for milk. We had to take it with us. It had to be taken care of. So we took our cow and let it graze up there.

Geraldine Chapman Buhler
Midvale

Preserving Butter

Butter may be preserved, if it is of first class quality, according to the [Utah Agricultural College] dairy expert.

Ada Peart, left, and Jerusha Bair hand wrap butter produced by the Utah Condensed Milk Company in Richmond, 1907. (Special Collections and Archives. Utah State University.)

Wash the milk out of the butter and place in crocks that have been scalded and allowed to dry without wiping. Make a brine strong enough to float an egg and let it cover and surround the butter. Keep in a cool place. Preserved this way, butter will be good for table use for two months, and for cooking purposes for six months. Another method is to pack the butter tightly in jars and cover with a thick layer of salt.

Utah Agricultural College
Extension Division
1917 (#21)

BUTTER FOR TRADE

As a child I very frequently went to Bishop George Robinson's store here in Laketown. His was a general mercantile business, too, and instead of having money to spend, in those days we would have an egg or two. And sometimes Grandmother Johnson would let cousin Willmirth and I each have a pound of her homemade butter, which we would take to Bishop Robinson's store. And we received 10¢ for the pound of butter. We sometimes bought cookies or a package of gum, but for most of the time it was candy.

Vella Satterthwaite
Laketown

Margarine Sacriledge

We used to sell milk and buy butter. We sold milk to the Sego plant, and when we sold milk, all we had to do — if I remember we had a code system. You put two little pebbles on top of the milk can, and that meant that you wanted two pounds of butter. However during the Depression, I can still see my dad with a churn, churning butter. We had plenty of butter because my father thought it was a sacriledge to use margarine. That just wasn't fit for human consumption as far as he was concerned.

Vernon Israelson

New York Cash Store

Mother had a big churn, what they call a barrel churn, about that big around and about that long, and she'd make up about seventy, seventy-five pounds of butter each week. And we'd take that in to customers. Some of it we'd sell to the stores. They had what they call "The New York Cash Store." That was one of our main customers where they handled most of our butter. Mother was very careful with it. They always would give her the best price for her butter. There was a Mrs. Reed, a little Swedish woman that lived on the river, and she used to keep her cream in a big well box. The flies were just terrible in those days. The only thing she could do was pick the flies out of the cream and churn it, and naturally there'd be a wing or a leg or something. And they told her, "Mrs. Reed, we just can't use your butter anymore." Well, she wanted to know what was the matter with it, so they said, "We seen pieces of flies."

"Well," she says, "I know better than that. I spent hours a-pickin' them flies out." But those were conditions in those days.

Harry Lunn
Ogden

Eggs for Trade

But what was best was the hard tack candy and the penny goods. And we always went to the store. You never did have money, but you always had a few chickens up in the coop, and Aunt Maud would give us a couple of eggs once or twice a week to take over to the store. And you'd trade the eggs for a little candy. And then they'd put the eggs up and put them in a container or a box and sell them back out to people in a paper sack. It didn't matter whether they were laid the same day as they were sold or not. So darn fussy nowadays that it's a pity.

Marion Olsen
Paradise

Cliff Dwellings Picnic

I do remember once — I can't remember whether I was four or six years old — we went on a picnic up to what they call the cliff dwellings. They was up above the old mill, up there in the canyon, before you get up the canyon very far. We went up there and was up in those cliff dwellings. I remember very plainly because . . . somebody was sup-

Lula Lane Keeffe displays the products of her Wellsville poultry farm, c. 1923. (Special Collections and Archives. Utah State University.)

posed to keep an eye on me, and I'd step or something and lost my balance. And I started rolling down that hill. It was just about, oh, [forty-five degrees] steep and about, oh, I'd say fifty yards or so down. And I just rolled head over heels, and my sister had just put an egg in her mouth. When she seen that, why, she blacked out. She'd swallowed the egg or got it caught in her mouth, and she passed out. And I went down there and hit in a clump of rocks, and blood was squirting from everywhere. And they thought I was killed. But it didn't seem to hurt me too much. It bloodied my nose, is about all that it done. So that's about the only picnic that I can remember.

Vernon D. Barney
Ogden

STORING EGGS

W. R. Graham reports the results of the following methods of preserving eggs: (1) Immersion in solutions of water glass [sodium silicate] of different strengths, (2) in lime solution, (3) coating with vaseline, (4) packing in salt, (5) packing in dry oats, (6) immersing in water glass and packing in egg cases after drying. The results obtained were in favor of lime water and water glass. Those coated with vaseline kept well but absorbed a very undesirable flavor of vaseline. Of those packed in salt only a small percentage were bad, but all had lost considerable from evaporation. Eggs packed in oats were musty and had evaporated fully as much as those packed in salt; those coated with pure water glass were fairly well preserved but lacked flavor.

Utah Agricultural College
Extension Division
1917 (#25)

If you set a hen on to hatch her eggs on a holiday or a Sunday, none of the chicks will turn out.

CROWING ROOSTER

I've always liked the farm, and I always liked the old cows. And I like the chickens, and I like the old rooster crowing in the morning, boy! Every time I wake up now, I listen with my ears to hear a rooster crow. Never could hear one down here.

Pierce Hardman
North Logan

CHILD'S PLAY

I let my children mostly live on the table or the cabinet top in the winter. They played there. It was cold on the [stone] floors. We'd sit around the kitchen fire or the front room stove with our feet up and read stories and spend the evening doing that. You just didn't play on the floor. Children couldn't sit on the floor. As soon as we moved in here with central heating, the floor is just as warm as any place to play, and the children sat on the floor all the time to play. But they never sat on the floor in a rock house. . . .

The children played games, and they popped corn. We always had apples to eat, and we sat around and ate apples. We read an awful lot of stories to the children, and they read. They played games just like they do now. They had their toy boxes and toys just like normal children. I had a big kitchen table cause I had so many men I had to cook for at onc time. I put the children on top of it, and they could play all kinds of games. They could play jacks just as well on the table as you can on the floor.

Mrs. Joseph Gilgen

Inside a photographer's studio, Mr. and Mrs. W. D. Goodwin pose as if picking apples, c. 1907. (Special Collections and Archives. Utah State University.)

FRIED APPLES

We used to go up to Bear Lake to my grandmother's, and she'd always make homemade doughnuts and fried apples. Just slice them up and fry them in a cube of butter and pour cinnamon and sugar on them. And they were wonderful. You sugar them as you fry them, and then you taste them, and if they're not sweet enough, you put more sugar on them. Sometimes she peeled them, and sometimes she didn't. It didn't matter. It depended on how fast we wanted them.

Mitzi Busath
Riverton

APPLE TREES

Yes, we'd sell the potatoes to grocerymen or to private homes. One time he took a load of potatoes in, and a lady had him carry them down in her storage. Then after a day or two she decided she didn't want them, so he went back and carried them back up. That's the thing: you're never sure of anything. We had a lot of apples until one year, 1916, they all froze — like they have this year. So the next year they were all pulled out with a Caterpillar tractor. He pushed them all out. He decided they weren't worth keeping. Too much work and no sale.

Adella Hurst

Chantilly Applesauce

5 tart apples
¼ cup fresh grated horseradish
2 tablespoons powdered sugar
Whipped cream

Core and steam apples. Rub them through a sieve. Add horseradish and powdered sugar. Chill and fold into an equal amount of whipped cream. Serve chilled.

Utah State Agricultural College
Extension Service
1939 (#NS 100)

Wages

He believed that the farm family should be self-supporting, and he was glad that he was a farmer so that we could make our living on the farm. He told all of us that he didn't want us to work away from home. We were asked sometimes to go and help pick fruit. Some of our friends were doing this, staying out of school to work. I said, "Oh, maybe I should work and earn some money to buy my clothes." But my parents didn't want us to miss any school. Father asked, "How much money will you earn?" I told him the amount being paid. He answered, "Well, I'll pay that amount. You're worth more than that to your mother and me by helping around the house and doing the farm chores!"

Beth Wyatt Winn
Salt Lake City

If you drop a dishrag, company will come before the next meal.

O. Larson peddles flowers, plants, and vegetables from a horse-drawn wagon in 1915. (Special Collections and Archives. Utah State University.)

Shipping Fruit

I think I told of the time when Dad sent seven car-loads of fruit back to Kansas and Missouri, and when it got there they prevented it from going to the market though we consigned it. The market back there, rather than having a glut on the market, dumped our fruit in the Missouri River, and it went down the river. He had to pay for the boxes, pay for the packing, and pay for the picking. That was seven carloads of fruit, and that made quite a dent in our pocketbook. It took years to scrape it out again.

Burton Tew
St. George

A Household Device for Summer Use: Iceless Refrigerator

We would call the attention of the Association to this refrigerator, which is manufactured by the Regal Manufacturing Company, Salt Lake City. We believe it to be well worth the while for housekeepers to learn more of this article. The points in its favor are:

It affords a medium in which foods may be kept in a wholesome condition without freezing.

It saves the ice bill.

It saves cleaning up after the ice man.

It keeps vegetables fresh and crisp.

It can be used for camping trips, being easily portable.

It allows all varieties of food to be stored at the same time without tainting one another. This is due to the constant passage of air.

It costs nothing to operate.

It may be operated with but little expenditure of trouble, since all that is needed is to keep the reservoir in the top filled with water, and the article itself where a current of air may reach it.

Its initial cost is small and is more than saved by the elimination of the ice bill.

Utah Agricultural College
Extension Division
1915 (#23 [24?])

Utah Apple Varieties

Ben Davis	Rome Beauty
Delicious	Wealthy
Gano	White Winter Pearmain
Grimes Golden	Winesap
Jonathan	Winter Banana
Northwestern Greening	Wolf River
Rhode Island Greening	Yellow Bellflower

Utah Agricultural College
Extension Division
1917 (#29)

Private Income

One Saturday Dad told me that I could have what peaches were left in the orchard that were left after he had harvested and sold all that he could sell. He gave me the

Peach pickers take a break in their labors near Brigham City,
c. 1907. (Compton Collection. Special Collections and Archives.
Utah State University.)

balance of the peaches that were over in the north field. Saturday afternoon I went back over and picked as hard as I could pick. After Dad went to Sunday School I went back and picked as hard as I could pick again.

I wanted a bicycle, and the only way I could get a bike—he wouldn't put up the money, and he didn't think a bike was necessary. I was in high school at that time. I went over and picked Saturday and Sunday. I sold $35 worth of peaches. We had taken them just out of the tops of the trees where someone had abandoned them. I sold enough peaches out of that orchard after Dad thought it was all gone to buy my bicycle from a day and a half's picking. That was big, big money and big, big fruit out of the tops of the trees. No one got hurt out of that fruit, and the next day when Dad learned that I had made that much money, he wanted half. My mother defended me and told him that, "it belonged to Burton, and I heard you give it to him."

Burton Tew
St. George

Weeding Strawberries

We always had strawberries. It was just a little space about as big as this platform here that we had strawberries. It was my job to weed and water the strawberries. I kept every weed out. I was about eleven years old.

Eva Campbell Bybee
Providence

CANNING PEACHES

Oh, yes, Mother bottled fruit. She always had a lot of peaches. Peaches was our main fruit. She would put up four and five hundred quarts of peaches, and there was many a time that I had to hurry home from school to help her put up the peaches. And a lot of times Aunt Lizzie would come over and help. She was a dear old soul. She'd come and help Mother because she knew that Mother was raising her family and had a lot to do, and she would come over and help us.

Sarah Wyatt Leishman
Nibley

DRIED STRAWBERRIES (SUN PRESERVES)

Select ripe, firm berries. Pick and preserve same day. Hull and rinse. Place in shallow platter in single layer; sprinkle sugar over them; pour over them 40 degrees syrup (1½ qts. sugar to 1 qt. water, boiled). Cover with glass dish or window pane. Allow to cook in hot sun 10 to 15 hours. Pack in glasses, jars, or cups; tie paper over tops. (Paraffin or sealing wax.) Keep in cool, dry place.

Utah Agricultural College
Extension Division
1915 (#14)

Conserve

    5 lbs. grapes
    5 lbs. sugar
    1 lb. raisins
    1 lb. shelled walnuts
    3 juicy oranges
    Spiced currants

Utah Agricultural College
Extension Division
1917 (#24)

Dried Fruit

He wanted to surprise Mom with the good quality of fruit. He used to have plums, also. We used to pit those plums and dry them. We had possibly twenty trees of plums and prunes. We'd split them and put them out to dry. We'd put them on the south side of the shed with a mosquito net on them to keep out the flies. We would put them on the south side of the shed. There we would dry a bushel of those to use for our winter fruit supply. Mother sold a lot of dried fruit.

Burton Tew
St. George

Grapes are harvested and boxed by families of pickers near
Brigham City, c. 1907. (Compton Collection. Special Collections
and Archives. Utah State University.)

BUYING PEARS

No, [we had] very few pears, because they would have to be boughten from the store. A lot of times we would have people come through from Provo and Brigham City with truck loads, and they would stop in, and Mother and Dad would buy whatever they felt they could afford at the time. And that was about the only way that we would get our pears.

Sarah Wyatt Leishman
Nibley

DRYING TOMATOES

Scald, cold dip, remove skin, halve, dip in boiling syrup (1 part Karo, 3 parts water), dry.

Co-operative Extension Work in Agriculture
and Home Economics, State of Utah
Utah Agricultural College
1918 (#27)

RIPE TOMATO PRESERVES

Take as much sugar as tomatoes and boil until you think done. It is best to peel the tomatoes without scalding them, as there is not so much water to boil down. Add a stick of cinnamon to flavor.

John Fitzgerald
Draper

Grape Catsup

2 quarts ripe grapes
Vinegar to cover
1 cup sugar
1 tablespoon cinnamon
1 tablespoon cloves
1 tablespoon allspice
¼ tablespoon cayenne

Cook grapes in vinegar till soft; strain, add sugar and spices, and cook till thick. If vinegar be very strong, use less and cook slowly to avoid burning.

Utah Agricultural College
Extension Division
1914 (#36)

Canning in Quantity

One thing that's really changed on this ranch is the amount of food that was consumed with these men and everything else. And we don't eat near as much now as we used to. We used to put up between 600 and 1,000 quarts of fruit here, and it'd generally about all be eaten up.

Loran Jackson

Fourteen-year-old Ruth Bybee displays an astonishing array of her work in the Boys' and Girls' Club Exhibit at the 1914 Utah State Fair. (Special Collections and Archives. Utah State University.)

Canning Aromas

We canned all our vegetables from the garden and the apples and plums from the orchard. Peaches, apricots, pears, and tomatoes were brought from Brigham City each fall. I remember helping can twelve bushels of peaches, six to eight bushels of tomatoes, besides gallons of pickles, ketchup, and chili sauce. The aroma of these pickles cooking on the wood stove or baking bread greeted the hoard of hungry kids returning from school even before we reached the gate.

Bernice Weston Sims

Brigham City Peaches

We used to go, see it was really a trip for us to go to Brigham. Dad would get the covered wagon and the horses and load us all in. We would take two days to go to Brigham and get a load of peaches and bring them back. He'd always take us over and get the peaches, and then we would take our food and camp out some place along the road. Then we would come back the next day. It was nothing for them to bring back ten and twelve and sometimes more bushels of peaches.

Sarah Wyatt Leishman
Nibley

Canning and Storing

In the evenings we would get together with the [quarry] men in their bunkhouse, which was just a short ways away, and they would tell stories to the boys. And there was always someone there that would have a musical instrument, and they would play, and we would have a jolly evening. I learned a lot of things while I was there. The one valuable thing that I learned while I was there was that RATS eat everything. I put up my fruit, and I paid a big price for my fruit because I did want to have my fruit to put up. I had no place to store it after I had put it up, so in paper boxes that the bottles come in, I sealed the boxes and put them under my bed so that I would have them. Later on, I knew that the fruit was spoiling. I opened it, and it was in the time when we had rubber to go around the bottles for the top. Somehow the rats had got in there and eaten all the rubber off the tops of the bottles, and I had nothing but spoiled fruit.

Clara Kelley
Providence

Cellar Supplies

Yes, we had a cellar under the house. [My wife], she was always putting up stuff to eat — gooseberries or something, anything she could find. She's pretty good, you know. If you don't think so, go down in the basement and look and see what she's got down there.

Pierce Hardman
North Logan

"Young town girl picking berries. Because of diversification of crops no migrant labor is needed or used in this section." Cache County, July 1940. (Photo by Russell Lee for Farm Security Administration, Library of Congress.)

RASPBERRY PICKERS

We had a half acre of raspberries up by our house. We got about 30¢ a case for them, and we had to pay the pickers a penny a cup to have them pick. By the time you buy your cups and your case, you'd make about 5¢ a case on them. And still we could save a dollar or two, you know, a few dollars. Like twenty dollars out of a season. Which now they want twenty dollars an hour. They won't even pick raspberries anymore cause they can't make three or four dollars. All the neighbors' kids would come and pick for us. The kids in our family all picked for just part of their family work. If we paid them, we wouldn't have nothing.

Agnes Merrill
Hyrum

SNITCHING GOOSEBERRIES

Oh, we raised everything. We always had a lot of potatoes. Dad was a firm believer in having plenty of potatoes, because he always said we could live on potatoes and gravy if we didn't have anything else. So we always had a nice crop of potatoes.

We always had a lot of carrots and onions, and oh — we had raspberries and gooseberries. Wonderful gooseberries. It was always fun to wait until the gooseberries got ripe and then go out and snitch them before Mom could get them to put them up, cause we loved them when they were nice and ripe.

Sarah Wyatt Leishman
Nibley

Berry Patches

Mother sold our fruit farm so that Carol and I and Myrtle—she called us her triplets because we were so close together—so that we could go to school. There was forty acres. Twenty acres of hay and then twenty acres of orchard. We planted lovely peach trees, and we planted apricot trees. And then raspberries. And we had those summer apples, those yellow summer apples. They were right above our raspberry patch, and we'd have to pick apples out of the raspberry patch. And we always had strawberries.

Eva Campbell Bybee
Providence

College Supplies

I've made gallons of tomato juice and fixed it so it'd keep. And then we'd always get about ten bushels of peaches. You know, just before John went on his mission, Valoy, this little girl that he married after, she was there with Amy. And they two peeled peaches, and John kept me in clean bottles, sterilized. And I had a whole stove—we were still burning wood then—and the next morning they went on their mission. They went off that day, and the next morning I counted the two-quart bottles that was there, and there was a hundred and twenty-three bottles of peaches. Just the two girls and John and I—just the four of us. I counted a hundred and twenty-three. We had a nice basement [to store them in]. Daddy built fruit shelves in the basement, and it was a nice place. And cool, you know. It kept good. And when the three boys went to school, went to college, three of them went to the A.C. there at Logan and always got their supplies from home. Fruit and everything. I canned cases and cases of string beans, and they'd just come home weekends and gather up what they wanted. Gather up whatever they wanted.

Eva Campbell Bybee
Providence

BASEMENT STORAGE

Part of the basement didn't have any cement in the bottom of it. It was more damp, you know. Damp enough so that the apples would keep. When they were going to spoil, why, I always got busy and made apple sauce. But as long as they'd keep hard, why, we'd just eat them that way.

Eva Campbell Bybee
Providence

SUET DUMPLINGS

½ as much suet as flour, one tablespoon sugar. Little salt, enough butter milk to make a thick batter 1 cup currants if wanted about ½ teaspoon of soda stir well put in sacks & boil an hour or more.

John Fitzgerald
Draper

An impressive array of goods were available from John
Thomassen, left, and his son Ferdinand in one corner of their
Richmond tinsmithing shop, about 1905. (Special Collections
and Archives. Utah State University.)

Quarry Cook

Different years were different. Most of the time we had about twenty men, but one year we had as high as thirty-five men to cook for. It wasn't hard, though, because we had all our vegetables brought up from Providence by the rock haulers. We went to the store twice in a month and got several hundred dollars' worth of food from the store, and that was the way we got along. But the haulers were always nice to bring fresh vegetables up and anything they could find for us. We did have one thing that was nice, and that was when the strawberries, raspberries, chokecherries, elderberries, and all the wild berries were in season. We would take our quart buckets and go out and pick enough for our dinner. When my husband would come home from work, he would take the bucket and go up where he knew they were and bring enough home for our supper and breakfast. This was very nice and seemed good.

When we first went to get our groceries, we went in a one-horse buggy. Then after a few years passed, we had a Dodge car that would pull up there, and we would take our groceries up in that.

Clara Kelley
Providence

Family Ranch

Dad lived there many years, and he had an opportunity to get some fruit orchards, and also he had a chance to buy a ten acre cherry orchard right by the pond on

Forest Street where he had the ice plant. It was quite a nice opening. But I guess the main thing was that he had bought the ranch, in the first place, to keep the family together. He called a family meeting, and there wasn't a single solitary one of us that wanted to be a farmer or a rancher. So he said, "Then we're not going to keep the ranch. I didn't get it for myself."

Joseph H. Watkins, Jr.

WATERMELON THIEF

I remember when I was a kid. I came home one night real late. I had been stealing watermelons with Johnny Gail. I didn't dare to come in the house until after dark. I came in through the braces of that house that he was building as I stood and hung around on the outside, not daring to come until it got so late that Mother would be anxious to have me come home. I knew it was late, and I wanted her to be glad enough to see me that she wouldn't whip me too much. I remember staying out in that old part of that house. I must have been seven or eight years old when that happened.

Burton Tew
St. George

WATERMELON PROTECTION

Another thing he done, he used to raise watermelons. And it got so the kids'd come and steal them. So every

If you swallow seeds, you'll get appendicitis.

Friends enjoy a watermelon feast in Morgan about 1910. (Special Collections and Archives. Utah State University.)

afternoon he'd go dig a hole in the ground out in the sand, and he'd put the watermelon down in there and cover the dirt over it. And then he'd go pull it up again. That's how he got them away from the kids.

Harvey Merrill
Hyrum

Melon Picking

And then I remember when I was about 17 — I believe it was about 17 — somebody wanted my brother Glen to come down to Green River and pick melons one fall, and so I asked him if I could go with him. . . . So we went. We got a ride to Price, and we hitched. Caught a ride on a freight train to Green River. That's the first time I ever rode on a freight train.

But anyway, why, we went down there, and this guy he was going to work for says, well he says, "I can use you, but I can't use your brother." Oh, that upset me, and I says, "Well, I'm going home then," and Glen says, "Well, if you can't work, I'll go home with you." And so old Joe says, "Well, listen. I've got a brother. Maybe he'd work for him."

So he took me over to Albert Allen's and Albert says, "Sure, I can use him." And so I worked for Albert.

We worked for two weeks until the melon peak was over. Then we caught a freight train and come home. I'd earned twenty dollars. I kept two dollars for tithing and two dollars for myself to spend and gave the rest of it to Marvin to go to school on.

Vernon D. Barney
Ogden

If one will eat a banana just before going to bed, he will dream in technicolor.

Babies are still bathed in a wash boiler at the recreated 1917
Jensen Historical Farm. Wellsville, 1986. (Photo by Jeannie
Thomas. R. V. Jensen Living Historical Farm.)

131 &

GUNPOWDER

For tonsillitis: Cut open bullets and remove the gunpowder. Grind it to a fine powder if necessary. Make a funnel out of paper and blow a small amount of gunpowder onto tonsils.

TURPENTINE

For sore throat, soak a feather in turpentine. Then paint the sore throat with it.

CONSTIPATION REMEDY

1 pound raisins
1 pound dates
1 pound prunes
1 pound figs
1 ounce ground senna

PARSLEY

To cure a bladder infection, eat parsley and drink a lot of water.

WORM CURE

Cut up hair and mix it with sugar and feed the mixture to the kids with worms.

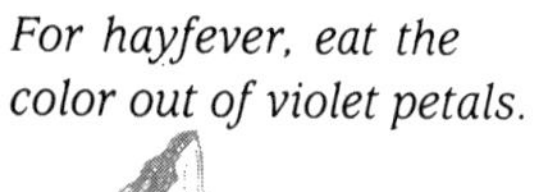

For hayfever, eat the color out of violet petals.

COUGH SYRUP RECIPE

Equal parts of honey, vinegar, whiskey, and linseed oil. Mix well and warm. Store in a bottle. Shake well before using. Dose: 1 teaspoon.

HONEY AND HONEYCOMB

For hayfever, all one has to do is eat a lot of honey and chew honeycomb. For bad cases, one may even want to put a small amount of honey in the nose.

CANKER MEDICINE

Well, I still remember a bottle of a mixture that was — I don't know who prepared, whether Mother had the combination of whatever they used — but it was in a little bottle, and it was called Canker Medicine. I don't know why everybody seemed to have canker or whether it was just called that. And every time they had something wrong with them, they gave them this Canker Medicine. I can still see it in the cupboard with my mother's handwriting on it, "Canker Medicine."

Helen Mabey Adams

TOOTHACHE CURE

Chew the root of blue flag iris to cure toothache.

For a cold, take sugar syrup and slice an onion in it. Simmer until the onions are tender. Drink it.

Advertisements cover the curtain of the Novelty Theatre stage,
a Logan vaudeville house, in 1904. (Special Collections and
Archives. Utah State University.)

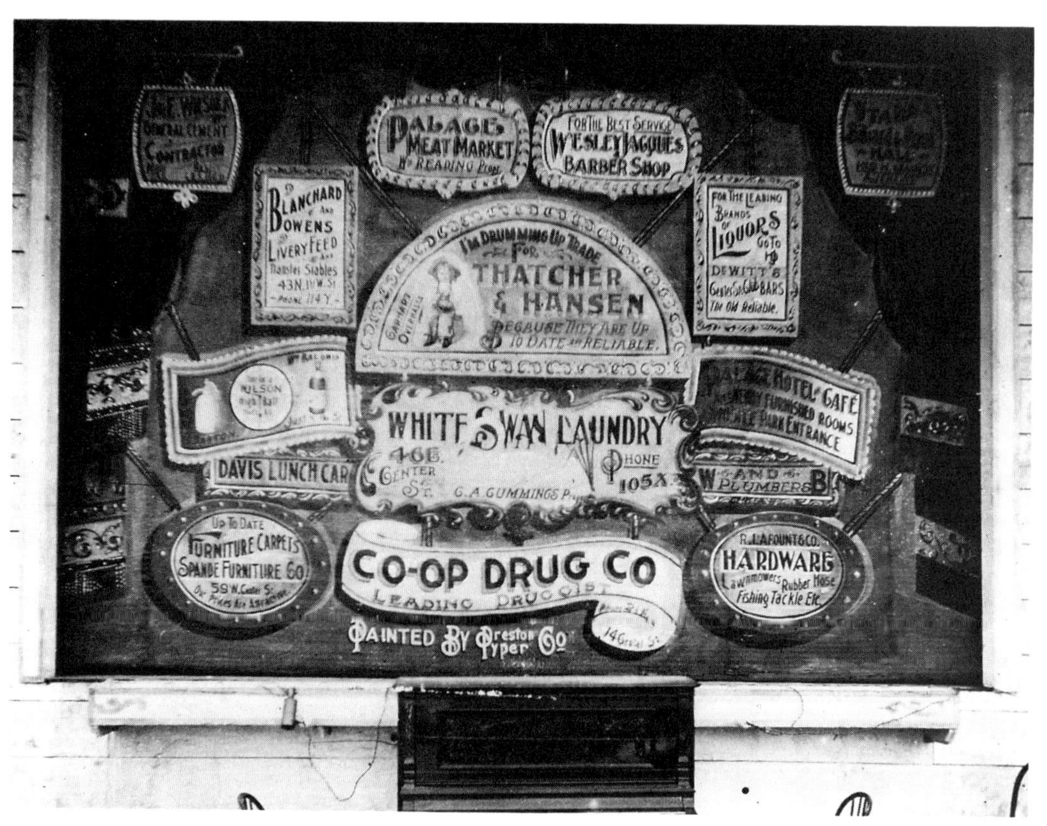

PALACE MEAT MARKET
FOR THE BEST SERVICE WESLEY JAQUES BARBER SHOP
BLANCHARD AND BOWENS LIVERY FEED
FOR THE LEADING BRANDS OF LIQUORS GO TO DEWITT'S
I'M DRUMMING UP TRADE FOR THATCHER & HANSEN BECAUSE THEY ARE UP TO DATE AND RELIABLE
WHITE SWAN LAUNDRY
PALACE HOTEL & CAFE
DAVIS LUNCH CAR
UP TO DATE FURNITURE CARPETS
CO-OP DRUG CO LEADING DRUGGIST
HARDWARE
PAINTED BY Preston Type Co

Sea Water

For arthritis, drink one cup of sea water from one mile out at sea.

Cures for Hoarseness

For hoarseness, suck a lump of sugar dipped in kerosene, drink sauerkraut juice, or wear your shirt backwards.

Frostbite Relief

Used internally, cayenne pepper helps relieve frostbite.

Cough Syrup

He had a bunch of us kids outside one time. We was going to get some cough syrup. One guy'd go in and get some cough syrup, and said he'd got a bad cough. Old Doc'd give him some cough syrup. He went in, and he come out. We were all drinking cough syrup, each one of us. So we went around, kept going around, so the doc got wise of it. I don't know what he gave us, but boy, we was all shaking. We never went after cough syrup no more. Oh, he used to pull the devil on the boys.

Howard T. Jones
Sunnyside

Cayenne and Honey

For a cold, take ⅛ teaspoon cayenne pepper and 1 tablespoon honey.

Cold Remedy

Dissolve a few drops of kerosene oil in sugar. Take internally.

Spring Tonic

Spring tonic is made from sulfur and molasses. We were supposed to take it every spring to build us up. I never had any, but Overlands did. I always shut my mouth.

Dema Nunley
Salt Lake City

Headache Cure

For headache, inhale the fumes of hot cider vinegar. Garlic can also be added.

Hayfever Relief

Hayfever may be treated by inhaling the vapors of a pint of hot water to which sixteen drops of creosote have been added. The nostrils may be sprayed with a solution

For colds: one pint or so of milk and one whole clove garlic. Simmer, strain, and drink.

of quinine (two grains to the ounce of water), while some persons find relief by inserting a tabloid of cocaine into the nostrils and letting it dissolve and exert its action on the nose membrane.

Newspaper clipping from
recipe notebook of
Nan Chipman
American Fork

Hiccough Cure

For hiccoughs: Put a teaspoonful of mustard in four ounces of boiling water. Drink when cool.

Beet Root Coffee

From the yellow beet root, sliced and dried in an oven and ground with a little foreign coffee.

Peppermint

Drink peppermint tea for health and energy.

Well Water

In the older days Mother tells a story. She used to have to walk down a little over a half mile to Aunt Cad Warren's place. They had a well. She would bring a bucket of water

Use catnip tea to quieten a baby.

"Running water in the home of a Mormon farmer. As these Mormon farmers live in communities, the problem of running water is easily solved." Santa Clara, October 1940. (Photo by Russell Lee for Farm Security Administration, Library of Congress.)

on one arm and Will in the other. While Dad was working in Springville — although they owned the farm, he was still making money working as a brick layer in Springville. Mother would have to go down there and get what water they wanted. She would go a half a mile and bring that water up.

Burton Tew
St. George

MOTHER'S COFFEE

When I was in the 5th grade, I lived about a block from the school, and the teacher would send me home almost every day to have my mother make her some coffee and bring back in a quart jar. In those days the teachers brought a sack lunch, and there was no machines with Coke in them, or root beer like they have now, or milk. So she just did it. I guess she liked my mother's coffee.

Iris Kunz Buhler
Midvale

INDIAN RATIONS

Getting into the summer part of those years, I recall having gone down to the agency toward the canyon on a few occasions with my mother to pick up rations. This was something the government had to do so far as the treaty of the Indians went. They had to see that the Indians had food. So this is one of the things, or one of the ways the Indians got their food. On this ration day we would go down, and of course you'd get bacon, a certain amount of bacon. Each family got an allotment depending on size of the family. Bacon, flour, raisins—wormy raisins, by the way. Wormy ones. And pretty good beans, and occasionally you'd get some fruit. It wouldn't be too much. You'd get coffee. It wasn't ground coffee. The beans had to be roasted before you could even grind it to make coffee. All this had to be done by hand, and if you didn't have a grinder, then you had to pound it to make it into coffee. Things went on like this.

LaMar LaRose

Root Beer

    5 gallons boiled water
    ½ of 25¢ of sassafras
    ¼ package hops
    1½ quarts honey, melted
    ½ bottle Hires Root Beer Extract
    1 cake yeast

Boil water, steep sassafras and hops, melt honey, strain and add to water. When luke warm add yeast and extract. Let stand overnight—stirring often—in a warm place and cork in morning. This will fill about 27 quart bottles.

Nan Chipman
American Fork

Water was critical to early Utahns for more than irrigating fields. A museum "farm wife" pauses during a long day's washing at the Jensen Historical Farm. Wellsville, 1986. (Photo by Jeannie Thomas. R. V. Jensen Living Historical Farm.)

141 ༀ

Dance Switch

But they had dances down there, and everybody would bring their babies. And of course, everybody had a great big wool shawl they'd wrap them up in. They had one little room in the back where they always put their babies on a bed in there. One night Tom Trout got in there and changed all the babies around in different shawls, and of course when the women went in to get their babies, they'd picked up their shawl, but they had somebody else's baby. When my mother got home, she had Arthur Loveridge. My brother Peck was real dark. He had big black eyes and was real dark, and Arthur Loveridge was redheaded and freckle-faced. And she had Arthur Loveridge for her baby in her shawl. So it took the women nearly all next day to go around and find their own babies.

Lydia Ann Taylor Skewes
Moab

Carrying Water

Water was a real problem, the nearest source being Fisher Point, three miles away. Every day Andy made a round trip, a journey of six miles, to get water for the household and to use in the garden — carrying it in two five-gallon cans strung on the ends of a pole across his shoulders.

Because the end of the world was coming by flood, Andy kept a hand-hewn Ponderosa Pine boat hung by ropes on the rear of his cabin. Above the boat was a butcher knife to cut the rope in order to make a speedy launch. Andy's mesa is between Fisher and Castle Valley and lies some 3,000 feet above the valley floor, so ol' Andy must have expected a real gurge.

Bill Buchanan

WINDMILL

Yes, [the creaking of the windmill is] a good sound, too. You know you're going to have water. After the electricity come, why, then you don't need the windmill. You could fix it up so you wouldn't need the wind then, see.

Pierce Hardman
North Logan

BATHING

The large downstairs room served as a kitchen, dining, living, as well as a bath which was a number three tub brought in and put behind the stove and filled with water carried from the ditch and heated on the stove. Each one would take their turns washing in the water which later was carried out by bucket.

Emma Walker
Moab

143 ﻌ

"Mormon children buying candy at a store." Mendon, August 1940. (Photo by Russell Lee for Farm Security Administration, Library of Congress.)

Grandma Alm's Shoebox Cake

    6 eggs beaten
    2 cups sugar
    2 cups milk
    2 teaspoons baking powder
    ½ pound grated coconut
    2 cups chopped walnuts
    1 cup pecans
    1 pound graham crackers, crushed
    ½ pound melted butter

Mix sugar and baking powder. Add eggs and milk. Mix by hand until the sugar doesn't feel grainy. Then add nuts, graham crackers, coconut, cooled melted butter. Stir well. Pour into waxed-paper-lined shoebox and cook at 250 degrees for 3½ hours.

Jan Anderson
Providence

Christmas Candy

Christmas was celebrated at our home. Christmas Eve we would make candy. And my father would always buy a box of oranges, and we'd hang our stockings up. And my mother would make homemade candy and put homemade candy and an orange in our stockings. And that was all we got for Christmas, but we seemed to be thankful and never wanted to have anything more because we knew our family was poor and couldn't afford it.

Iris Kunz Buhler
Midvale

Candy Treat

We always had plenty of honey because we had a large hive of bees. All of the kids from blocks away can remember coming over to our house and sampling some of our honey. The honeycomb tasted just like candy, so sweet and good that all of the kids would come over to our house just to sample it. I can remember when I went to school there would always be a piece of candy wrapped up for me in my pocket. And sometimes my mother would put a dime in my pocket for me. She was a very hard worker, and all of my memories of her reflect back to what a wonderful person she was.

Joseph Christian Jacobsen
Logan

Jelly Beans

He ran a little candy store alongside his post office, and it was separate from his house. He used to have to come from the house over into it. The kids'd go in there and buy candy, and I remember one day I went in there, and there was a kid that was buying some jelly beans. I was watching him. I couldn't get my mail because he was busy, and I was watching him. He weighed these jelly beans out. He wanted a nickel's worth of jelly beans, and he'd weigh them out. I seen him bite a jelly bean in two to make the weight right. He was noted for that. He was stingy, but he was accurate.

Fred Kuhni
Heber City

"Canned goods and flour stored for winter use by a Mormon family." Santa Clara, October 1940. (Photo by Russell Lee for Farm Security Administration, Library of Congress.)

GRANDMOTHER'S COOKIES

[My grandmother] made raisin cookies that were about as hard as the back of your head and always had burned raisins in them. And about half enough sugar, but when you're little, they fill your empty stomachs.

Alan Godfrey
Garland

CHERRY COOKIES

1¼ cups sugar
¾ cup shortening
2 eggs
1 cup sour cherries
¼ cup juice
1 teaspoon soda
½ teaspoon salt
3 cups flour

Eulalia Welch Sorensen
Mendon

PIE MAKER

I guess the thing I like most of all is when my dad makes pies. He's the pie maker in the family, and he usually makes very good apple pie. I don't think there's any secret tricks. Use Jonathan apples. That's the only trick.

Dale Busath
Riverton

P ATIENCE

The name of this caramel candy is apt. It's at least an hour's project but well worth the effort. When combining the first two ingredients, be sure to heat the milk and stir the caramelized sugar into the milk—not the other way around.

1 cup milk (first then sugar)
1 cup carmelized sugar
1 cup cream
2 cups sugar
Stir constantly until it forms soft ball.
1 tablespoon vanilla

Idell Jensen Matthews
Logan

R AISIN P IE

We entertained ourselves because we lived too far from neighbors to go very often to see them. The girls played with their dolls. We had beautiful Christmases, and the girls always played with the dolls. Then in the summers when it was nice so we could go outdoors to play, we made mud pies. My father had sheep, so that gave us raisins to put into our pies.

Lucille Moffat Thornock
Randolf

Old Maid

As I grew up, if you took the last piece from a plate (as I remember, baked goods), someone would remark, "You will be an old maid."

Alta Fife
Logan

Snow Ice Cream

We lived on a ranch in Meadowville, and the winters were very severe. Father always kept a shovel inside the door, as the drifts were often as high as the outside buildings. He would dig his path to the barn each day. I can just hear the wind blowing and see the snow piling up. We made ice cream out of snow, sugar, and vanilla.

Lucille Moffat Thornock
Randolph

Snow or Ice

When we wanted to make ice cream — I had a great big ice cream freezer — and when we wanted to make ice cream, we'd go up in the hills and get some snow. Or else go and get some ice, but we never did have ice of our own.

Eva Campbell Bybee
Providence

Utah Construction Company ranch workers unload ice from a truck into an ice house, 1918. (Special Collections and Archives. Utah State University.)

Frozen River

I remember one year they used to cross on the ice. I don't know why it was, but the river always froze over, and the minute we got refrigerators, it quit and never has frozen over since. So things move in mysterious ways, I guess. But anyway, we used to haul ice.

Lydia Ann Taylor Skewes
Moab

Birthday Cake

My cousin Wilford and I celebrated our birthdays together sometimes since they were on the same day, the 16th of September. When I was about ten and he twelve, our sisters gave us a combined party at our home. We played games on the lawn. Kick the Can was the most popular one. Cake and lemonade was served under the large shade trees.

Beth Wyatt Winn
Salt Lake City

A girl that whistles and a hen that crows Will make her living wherever she goes.

Angel Food Doughnuts

    1 cup mashed potatoes
    Scald 1 quart milk
    ¾ cup shortening
    12 tablespoons sugar
    1 cup cold water
    Mix together, cool till lukewarm.

    Add:
    5 yeast cakes
    4 eggs
    1 tablespoon salt
    10 cups flour

Let rise. Push down. Roll out ¼ inch thick. Cook in oil. Frosting: 2 cups powdered sugar, ¼ cup boiling water, 1 teaspoon vanilla.

Lona Stevens
Clearfield

Rice Pudding

With a large family, my mother's specialty was a rice pudding and a bread pudding. We would take our cup of rice and put it in milk and put it in the round pan and put it in the old time oven and put sugar and maybe some raisins in it and let that cook for our dinner. And as that would brown on top, we would turn that in, and it would give you your flavoring of a caramel flavor. That was her specialty. I've kind of outgrown a lot of this cooking. There's too many restaurants around.

Maxine Rawlins
Cove

Norbert Dupin, left, and Mary Zagar Dupin tend the counter in
Spring Glen's Dupin Store, 1937. (Special Collections and
Archives. Utah State University.)

Chocolate-Marshmallow Eggs

2 Knox gelatin packages
6 tablespoons water
Allow gelatin to soak in water

1½ cups sugar
½ cup water
Bring to a boil. Add the gelatin, a dash of salt, flavor, and color. Beat with mixmaster for 7 minutes. Put in flour mold. Dip in chocolate and decorate.

Flour mold: Fill a dripper pan half full of flour. Press real eggs into the flour to make half-egg impressions. Pour the marshmallow into these shapes. Cool.

Betty Webb
Logan

Bonner Mercantile

Some jobs that [my father] done managed to gather up a little cash to save enough to take us kids to the store. Whenever we bought clothes or anything, we always went to the store with him to get just what we wanted. Used to go up to old Bonner Mercantile, George Bonner. He was very, very well treated. Whenever he went in there with us kids to buy us clothes or something, none of us ever went out of there without a sack of candy in our hand.

Fred Kuhni
Heber City

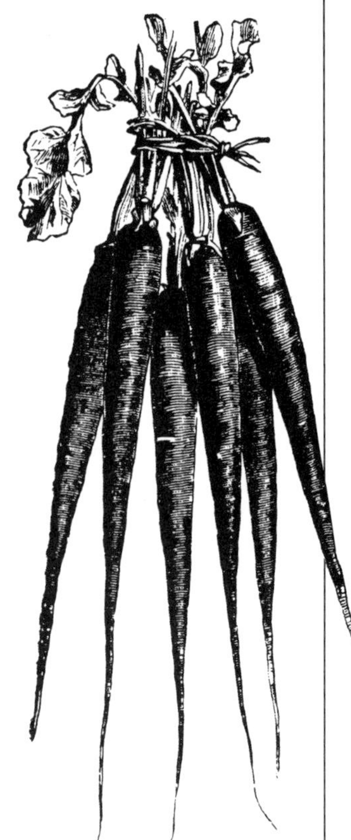

Mrs. Grover's Pudding

Juice of any kind of fruit.
Thicken with cornstarch.
Serve with whipped cream.

Eulalia Welch Sorensen
Mendon

Carrot Pudding

1 cup grated carrot
1 cup grated potato
1 cup grease
2 cups flour
1 cup raisins
1 cup currants
1 teaspoon soda
1 egg
Spices to suit taste
Brown sugar

Idell Jensen Matthews
Logan

Beehives

When someone died the others in the family would drape a piece of black material over their beehives so that the bees wouldn't desert the hive and the honey would be saved.

Gentlemen show off a crop of fruit and cabbages, c. 1907. (Compton Collection. Special Collections and Archives. Utah State University.)

Eggless Fruit Cake

    1 cup sugar
    1½ cup water
    1 cup seeded raisins
    ⅓ cup shortening
    1 teaspoon salt
    1 teaspoon nutmeg
    1 teaspoon cinnamon
    1 cup flour
    1 cup graham
    5 teaspoons baking powder

Boil sugar, water, fruit, shortening, salt, and spices together for three minutes. Cool. Add other ingredients, a wee bit more flour, and nuts.

Idell Jensen Matthews
Logan

Stuffed Raisins for Luncheon and Teas

Blanche almonds. Take large Muscat raisins and take out seeds. Slit raisins slightly and insert almonds and draw skin around to cover opening.

Idell Jensen Matthews
Logan

Pies and Noodles

Well, the church, of course, is the center of activity in any Mormon community—the church influence. They always had a basement in the church that was called the "vestry," I think. That was a large room with a polished oak or maple floor. That was where they held the church dances. . . . In these dances they had an intermission in the middle of the dance and would have a little refreshment. On those occasions the Relief Society would prepare the food. It was good. I can remember one year when I was a little kid—maybe four or five—about 1900 or around there, some of these pranksters stole all the pies and noodles. In that early time, the kids who did something like that, . . . they'd have to get up in church and ask forgiveness.

Vernon Ward
Ogden

Dance Music

We had a dance on Christmas Night And New years also our Meeting house was verey Small 14 × 16 And our Music was verey Scarce onley one Violine And there was to Maney for the house So we devided up And one part went to Bro John Maughans house Bro to Bishop Wm H Maughan And I was one that went to John Maughans house but when we got there we had No Music So I was Calld to Make Music for the dance being a good Wistler I had to do My best John Maughan And Bro Frank Gunnel did the Calling And we had a good time all the Same but in those days I Could Make as good Music as a flute or Pickalo

Charles Ramsden Bailey

Food and nutrition students perfect fruit-canning techniques at
the Utah Agricultural College about 1908. (Special Collections
and Archives. Utah State University.)

160

Mr. Poppinga's Cheese Fudge

Melt together:
1 pound Velveeta cheese
1 pound butter
Remove from heat and stir in:
4 pounds powdered sugar
1 cup cocoa
1 tablespoon vanilla
Nuts

Spread in a 9 × 13 inch pan and cool.

Jan Anderson
Providence

Potato Chip Cookies

1 pound butter or margarine
1 cup sugar
3 cups flour
2 cups crushed potato chips
1 cup chopped pecans
1 tablespoon vanilla
Confectioners sugar

Cream butter, then add sugar gradually, and beat well. Add flour and remaining ingredients, except confectioners sugar. Chill dough for 15 to 30 minutes. Shape dough into small balls and place on ungreased baking sheets. Flatten each with a fork dipped in cold water. Chill dough between batches to make it easier to handle. Bake in a preheated

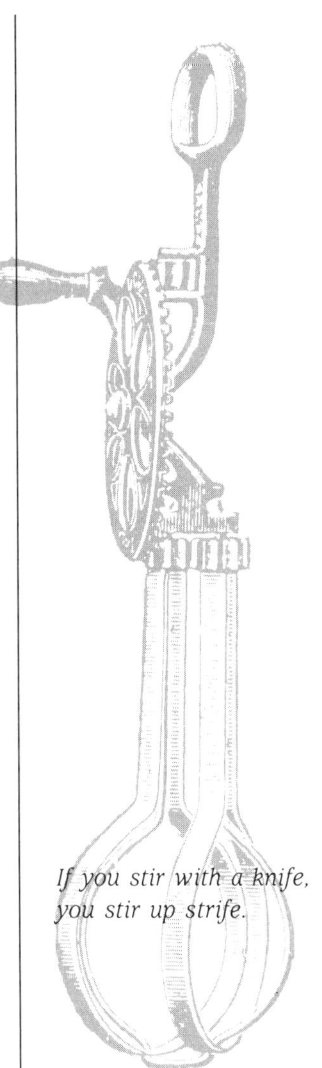

oven at 325 degrees for 20 minutes. Cool. Sprinkle confectioners sugar on top. If stored airtight, they keep well up to 3 weeks.

Sharon Allen
Millville

Lumpy Dick

Harvey: Thickened milk. That's what you call Lumpy Dick.

Agnes: About a quart and a half of milk. You bring that to a boil. In the meantime, while that's getting ready to boil, you put one cup of flour and a half a teaspoon of salt, and you take an egg and beat that, and you put that in this flour. And then just keep stirring it quickly with a fork until it all crumbles in little crumbles. And when the milk comes to a boil, you turn the stove off, and you put that in and give it a couple of stirs and put the lid on and let it set. And it's just like, well, I used to do it for my kids, and I called it imitation rice. We always used butter and sugar and cinnamon and cream. He wants salt and butter.

Harvey: At our home we never used sugar. It was just a regular meal like they do—sit down, and you don't put sugar on your potatoes or eggs or anything like that. That's the way this was. We used to have a lot of that every night. My father liked that, and we liked it. We were raised on it. We called it Lumpy Dick. Reason is the name of it is Thickened Milk. That's the real name, but they nicknamed it Lumpy Dick. It all comes out in little lumps. It's much better if it all comes out in little lumps than if it comes out like gravy. Much better. My mother was just perfect at making it. We used to have it two or three times a week at night.

Harvey and Agnes Merrill
Hyrum

CHRISTMAS CAKE

2 cups brown sugar
½ pound butter
4 eggs
1 cup molasses
1 tablespoon soda
1 cup coffee
1 cup jelly
1½ pounds dates
2 packages raisins
Cherries candied
Orange peel
1 pound nuts
1 teaspoon cinnamon
1 tablespoon allspice
Flour to make very stiff
Bake 3 hours

Eulalia Welch Sorensen
Mendon

Local producers deliver their milk to the Richfield Creamery, c. 1890–1900. (Special Collections and Archives. Utah State University.)

Store on Wheels

We had a store on wheels. Brother Johnny Baxter owned a little store in town, him and Joe Brown. They fixed up a sheep wagon there, cleaned it all up and filled that full of store goods, yardages and goods that people would need. Once a week they would come down, and we'd hear the bell ringing. They had a bell up on the top of it. They just kept pulling the string and ringing the bell. I would say, "Mother, here comes the store on wheels." I'd have the eggs all gathered for so long and cleaned up nice. I had the privilege to go in the store with my mother and help her pick out different things. We would pay for them in eggs and a little money. We'd save our nickels and dimes. We'd always come out of there with some hard tack candy. It was really something when the store on wheels came down then.

Annie Leishman
Wellsville

Cookie Jar

We always found something nice to eat when we went to Mother's. And our kids when they come home now, our grandkids, if we don't have cookies in the cookie jar, we're scolded. First thing they look at. They walk right in the kitchen door and right to the cookie jar. One day we weren't there when they came, and when they came, I happened to have graham crackers in the cookie jar. My grand-daughter wrote me and said, "Grandma, since when do you have graham crackers in the cookie jar?" So I don't do that anymore. I always have cookies. I keep up my reputation.

Esther Morgan
Logan

MEMORIES

And there was always a big crowd went to the dances. And they didn't just sit around and listen to the music. Everybody danced. All the old and the young and everyone else. As soon as the music started, the floor was loaded with people. The kids nowadays don't know what fun is at a dance. Everybody danced and really had a good time. The neighbors all, like I mentioned before, they liked a really good time. They liked to associate together. They had genuine fun that you like to remember. Some of the things now that they call fun, I guess a lot of them don't want to remember. That's the way I look at it. I look back on my boyhood days and the good times we had with our neighbors and friends, and it's a happy memory. I think the passing of time is a kind of a sad thing, but if you've got a few happy memories to mix in with your thoughts, it would kind of help take the sting off of old age, if nothing else.

Earl J. Stuart
Randolph

Sources

Sources of written materials in the text can be identified using the following source lists.

The first list includes all materials from interviews, notebooks, diaries, and other personal sources. In this list, each source that is available in the Special Collections and Archives Division of Utah State University's Merrill Library is indicated with an asterisk. Items not designated with an asterisk are in personal collections.

The second list includes all items quoted from publications of the Utah State University Extension Service and Agricultural Experiment Station. All of these materials are available in the U.S.U. Special Collections and Archives.

Sources of photographs are indicated in the photo captions.

Any item the origin of which is not identified in the text is from the U.S.U. Fife Folklore Archives.

Informant	Source	Date	Informant's Residence	Informant's Year of Birth or Age at Interview
Adams, Helen Mabey	*Interview by Jane Adams			
Allen, Sharon	Conversation with Jan Anderson	2/13/87	Millville	
Anderson, A.J.	*Interview by John Ericksen	12/24/75	Fairview	
Anderson, Jan	Personal recipe file		Providence	1952
Andrus, Gordon	Interview by Jan Anderson	8/16/86	Logan	age 26
Bailey, Charles Ramsden	*Autobiography	1839–1910		
Barker, Jessie	*Interview by Lynn H. Polson	1/1/74	Newton	1892
Barney, Marvin	*Interview by Ronald O. Barney	2/21/76	Ogden	1912
Barney, Vernon D.	*Interview by Ronald O. Barney	1/18/76	Ogden	1918
Bartlett, Ross	*Interview by Craig Fuller		Vernal	
Borrowman, John	*Journal of John Borrowman			

---

*Available in Special Collections and Archives
Merrill Library, Utah State University

Informant	Source	Date	Informant's Residence	Informant's Year of Birth or Age at Interview
Buchanan, Bill	*Interview by Laura Bailey	5/23/74		
Buhler, Geraldine D. Chapman	*Interview by Christine Buhler	3/6/77	Midvale	1921
Buhler, Iris Kunz	*Interview by Christine Buhler	2/18/77	Midvale	1899
Bundy, Genevieve	Recipe handouts from Southern Utah Folklife Festival, Utah Arts Council	1979	Dixie	
Busath, Dale	Interview by Jan Anderson	8/16/86	Riverton	age 28
Busath, Mitzi	Interview by Jan Anderson	8/16/86	Riverton	age 29
Bybee, Eva Campbell	Interview by Jan Anderson	8/16/86	Providence	age 92
Chipman, Nan	Nan Booth interview by Jan Anderson	12/3/86	American Fork	1865
Fife, Alta	Interview by Jan Anderson	1986	Logan	age 74
Fitzgerald, John	*Notebook	1885–98?	Draper	
Gilgen, Mrs. Joseph	*Interview by Kevin Anderson	5/25/72		
Godfrey, Alan	Interview by Jan Anderson	8/16/86	Garland	age 35
Gonzoles, Ernestine	Recipe handouts from Living Traditions Festival, Utah Arts Council	1986	Ephriam	
Griffin, Shirley M.	Interview by Jan Anderson	8/16/86	Brigham City	age 50
Hardman, Pierce	*Interview by Charles S. Peterson	1/16/73	North Logan	1880
Hogan, Goudy E.	*Diary	1837–80		
Hood, Robert	Interview by Jan Anderson	8/16/86	Midvale	age 21
Hurst, Adella	*Interview by Kevin Anderson	1/24/75		
Israelson, Eva Mae	*Interview by Kevin Anderson	5/17/72	North Logan	
Israelson, Vernon	*Interview by Kevin Anderson	1972		
Izatt, Barbara	*Bernice Weston Sims interview by M.E. Izatt	5/27/73		

Informant	Source	Date	Informant's Residence	Informant's Year of Birth or Age at Interview
Jackson, Loran	*Interview by Willa T. Kennedy	7/15/75		
Jacobsen, Joseph Christian	*Interview by Marie F. Olsen	1/17/80	Logan	
Jones, Howard T.	*Interview by J. Glenn Preston	1974	Sunnyside	1900
Kelley, Clara	*Interview by Marie F. Olsen	2/26/77	Providence	
Knighton, Lester	*Interview by Jill Brown	1/22/75?	Bountiful	1909
Kuhni, Fred	*Interview by Craig Fuller	7/23/74	Heber City	1897
Lamborn, Ray	*Interview by Reed Eborn	5/3/75		
LaRose, LaMar	*Interview by Cherri Silvestro			
Larsen, Ambrious	*Interview by Craig Fuller	11/6/74	Cove	1898
Leishman, Annie	*Interview by Sandra Bailey	5/17/73	Wellsville	1891
Leishman, Sarah Wyatt	*Interview by Mary Evelyn Izatt	7/5/74	Nibley	1911
Lichfield, Walt	Conversation with Jan Anderson	12/11/86	Providence	age 59
Lunn, Harry	*Interview by Craig Fuller	10/25/74	Ogden	1884
Matthews, Idell Jensen	Recipe notebook		Logan	1900
Merrill, Agnes	Interview by Jan Anderson	8/16/86	Hyrum	age 77
Merrill, Harvey	Interview by Jan Anderson	8/16/86	Hyrum	age 94
Morgan, Esther	Interview by Jan Anderson	8/16/86	Logan	age 74
Morgan, Stanley	Interview by Jan Anderson	8/16/86	Logan	age 80
Nunley, Dema	*Interview by Kristine Beckstrom		Salt Lake City	age 60
Olsen, Arlynn	*Interview by Pat Snowball	4/5/72	Paradise	
Olsen, Lloyd	*Interview by Pat Snowball	4/5/72	Paradise	
Olsen, Marion	*Interview by Paul Willie	3/8/76	Paradise	
Rawlins, Maxine	Interview by Jan Anderson	8/16/86	Cove	age 67
Rawlins, Reginald	Interview by Jan Anderson	8/16/86	Cove	age 73
Sanders, Janice	Recipe handouts from Southern Utah Folklife Festival, Utah Arts Council	1979		

*Available in Special Collections and Archives
Merrill Library, Utah State University

Informant	Source	Date	Informant's Residence	Informant's Year of Birth or Age at Interview
Sanders, Lynn	Recipe handouts from Southern Utah Folklife Festival, Utah Arts Council	1979		
Satterthwaite, Vella	*Interview by Maleta Robinson	5/9/75	Laketown	1900
Scott, Vaughn	*Interview by Rosemarie Page	1972		
Sharp, David	*Interview by Charles S. Peterson	5/18/72		1888
Skewes, Lydia Ann Taylor	*Interview by Betty Tibbets Farrow	4/29/74	Moab	1885
Simmonds, Lloyd	*Interview by Paul Willie	2/5/76	Trenton	
Sims, Bernice Weston	*Interview by Mary Evelyn Izatt	5/27/73		
Smith, Phebe	*Interview by Willa Kennedy	4/24/75	Randolph	1889
Sorensen, Eulalia Welch	Recipe notebook	1913–65	Logan	1890
Sorensen, Mary Jacobsen	Edith Morgan interview by Jan Anderson	12/30/86	Mendon	1850
Spencer, John	*Interview by Orlo Spencer	4/12/75	Fort Duchesne	1886
Stevens, Lona	Alta Fife interview by Jan Anderson	1986	Clearfield	age 76
Stuart, J. Earl	*Interview by Willa T. Kennedy	5/27/75	Randolph	
Tew, Burton	*Interview by Charles S. Peterson	11/25/72 and 11/26/72	St. George	1900
Thornock, Lucille Moffat	*Interview by Willa T. Kennedy	6/25/75	Randolph	1891
Toelken, Miiko	Interview by Jan Anderson	1/3/87	Logan	age 50
Vilos, Katherine J.	*Interview by Jim Vilos	11/5/72		
Walker, Emma	*Interview by Janice Gilliland	5/19/74	Moab	
Ward, Vernon	*Interview by Teddy Griffith	1/25/73	Ogden	
Watkins, Joseph H., Jr.	*Interview by Charles S. Peterson	6/7/74		1886

*Available in Special Collections and Archives
Merrill Library, Utah State University

Informant	Source	Date	Informant's Residence	Informant's Year of Birth or Age at Interview
Webb, Betty	Personal recipe file	1987	Logan	1935
Weston, Herbert R.	*Interview by Randy Weston	1/11/78	Logan	
Whiting, Heber	*Interview by Bruce Johnson	2/12/77		1901
Winder, Daniel	Recipe handouts from Southern Utah Folklife Festival, Utah Arts Council	1979	Springdale	
Winn, Beth Wyatt	*Interview by Charles S. Peterson	7/12/73	Salt Lake City	
Woodruff, Wilford	*Wilford Woodruff's Journal edited by Scott G. Kennedy; Signature Books	1833–98		

---

*Available in Special Collections and Archives
Merrill Library, Utah State University*

Utah State University Agricultural Experiment Station and Cooperative Extension Service Circulars and Bulletins

Year	Volume	Number	Title	Author	Agency
1906		96	Care of Milk on the Farm and the Manufacture of Butter and Cheese		Experiment Station of the Ag. College of Utah.
1912	1	6 [7?]	Labor Saving Devices for the Farm Home	Leah D. Widtsoe	Utah Ag. College Experiment Station. Extension Division.
1914	11 [2?]	36	Program Leaflet of Home Economics Associations		Utah Ag. College. Extension Division.
1915	3	14	Canning Club Instructions	J.C. Hogenson	Utah Ag. College. Extension Division.

Year	Volume	Number	Title	Author	Agency
1915	3	23 [24?]	Program Leaflet of Home Ec. Assns.		Utah Ag. College. Extension Division.
1917	5	18	Preservation of Fruits, Vegetables, and Meats	Gertrude McCheyne and J.C. Hogenson	Utah Ag. College. Extension Division.
1917	5	21	Program Leaflet of Home Ec. Assns.	Gertrude McCheyne	Utah Ag. College. Extension Division.
1917	5	24	Program Leaflet of Home Ec. Assns.	Gertrude McCheyne and Hortense White	Utah Ag. College. Extension Division.
1917		25	Preserving Eggs for the Home	Byron Alder	Utah Ag. College. Experiment Station.
1917	5	25	Program Leaflet of Home Ec. Assns. Topics: Storage of Winter Vegetables, Dairy Products in the Diet	Gertrude McCheyne and Hortense White	Utah Ag. College. Extension Division.
1917	5	29	Program Leaflet for Home Ec. Assns. Topics: Apples, the Best Varieties for All Uses, Their Food Value, Recipes	Gertrude McCheyne and Hortense White	Utah Ag. College. Extension Division.
1918	6	12	Sow and Litter Project for Boys' and Girls' Clubs	J.C. Hogenson and E.W. Stephens	Utah Ag. College. Extension Division.
1918	6	20	Program Leaflet of Home Ec. Assns. Topics: Jelly Making; Fruit Leathers	Gertrude McCheyne and Hortense White	Utah Ag. College. Extension Division.
1918	6	21	Program Leaflet of Home Ec. Assns. Topics: Baking Powder and Yeast War Breads; Salting of Vegetables; Saving of Sugar	Gertrude McCheyne and Hortense White	Utah Ag. College. Extension Division.

Year	Volume	Number	Title	Author	Agency
1918	6	27	Conservation Pointers for Boys' and Girls' Clubs	J.C. Hogenson, compiler	Co-operative Extension Work in Agriculture and Home Ec., State of Utah. Utah Ag. Coll.
1918	6	30	Program Leaflet of Home Ec. Assns. Topics: Farm Bureau and the Home; What It Takes to Feed and Clothe Our Soldiers; Latest Flour Regulations; Use Light Weight Meats	Gertrude McCheyne and Hortense White	Utah Ag. College. Extension Division.
[1920]	8	2	Important Factors in Successful Dry Farming in Utah	John T. Caine III	Agricultural College of Utah. Extension Division.
1929		80	Domestic Slaughtering, Cutting, and Curing of Pork	Harry H. Smith	Utah State Ag. College. Agricultural Experiment Station.
1930		NS 24	The Day's Food Supply. Helps to 4-H Leaders on How to Make the Best Foods Better	Elna Miller	Utah State Ag. College. Extension Service.
1934		NS 63	Safe Home Practices for Food Preservation	Elna Miller	Utah State Ag. College. Extension Service.
1934		104	Types of Greens and Pot-Herbs Used in Rural Utah Homes	Almeda Perry Brown	Utah State Ag. College. Utah Agricultural Experiment Station.
1935		NS 80	Adequate Lunches for School Children	Elna Miller	Utah State Ag. College. Extension Service.
1939		NS 100	Let's Eat Utah Apples!		Utah State Ag. College. Extension Service.
[1948]		170	Learn About Luncheons. 4-H Foods Project— Phase II.		U.S.A.C. Extension Service.

Suggestions for Further Reading

A number of delectable books are available for lovers of Utah cooking—and eating.

Lion House Recipes, compiled by Helen Thackeray (Salt Lake City: Deseret Book Co., 1980), is a favorite of Mormon cooks because of its connection with Brigham Young's family home, the Lion House. The recipes are from the cooks who have prepared the dishes served in the Lion House cafeteria since the home became a tourist stop.

For a taste of frontier trail cooking, *The Great American Dutch Oven Cook Book*, edited by Dick Michaud, Mike Kohler, et al. (Logan, UT: Festival of the American West, no date), offers recipes for cooking in the lidded cast iron pot that cooked the stews, dinners, and breads of many a pioneer or cowboy cook.

Like church congregations across the country, Utah's Mormon wards and congregations of other faiths have often assembled cookbooks containing the members' personal specialties. These are frequently locally produced and available only through church members. Church cookbooks provide an insight into the dishes popular today and may or may not include historical recipes as well.

A large number of commercially produced Utah cookbooks are available, too. By and large these include modern recipes only—from Shrimp Jambalaya to Spaghetti Primavera. Some good examples of this group are *A Pinch of Salt Lake Cook Book* (Salt Lake City: The Junior League of Salt Lake City, 1986) with its beautiful color photos; *Mormon Country Cookbook* by Winnifred C. Jardine (Salt Lake City: Bookcraft, 1980), food editor of the *Deseret News* for over thirty years; *With Singleness of Heart: Recipes for Sunday Meals* by Helen R. Bateman, JoAnn E. Hickman, and Jane S. Eddington (Salt Lake City: Deseret Book Co., 1984) with ideas for Sunday family mealtimes; and *The Mormon Family Cook Book* by Helen Thackeray, Beth Nelms Brown, and Maurine Hegsted (Salt Lake City: Deseret Book Co., 1982), also with a family emphasis.

The importance of food preservation and storage in the Mormon culture is illustrated by the wide range of preservation and emergency food handbooks produced by Utah authors. These often include topics such as what, how, and how much to store for a year's food supply, control of rodents, recipes for preparing tasty dishes from emergency rations, and so forth. This group includes titles like *Making the Best of Basics: Family Preparedness Handbook* by James Talmadge Stevens (Salt Lake City: Peton Corp., 1974); *Just in Case: A Manual of Home Preparedness* by Barbara S. Salsbury (Salt Lake City: Bookcraft, 1975); and *Survival Family: How One Family Prepared for and Lived One Year of Experi-*

mental Disaster! by Mary and Tom Bergman (Salt Lake City: Hawkes Publishing, Inc., 1977).

For an insight into Mormon culture and life, Wallace Stegner's *Mormon Country* (New York: Duell, Sloan, and Pierce, 1942) with its essays on historical as well as modern aspects of life is such enjoyable reading, it's still hard to beat. *Deseret 1776–1976: A Bicentennial Illustrated History of Utah* (Salt Lake City: Deseret News Publishing Co., 1975) is a basic introduction to the history of the state with an easy-to-read text and many illustrations. ("State of Deseret" was the first state name used by the early settlers. "Deseret" is a word from the *Book of Mormon* meaning "honeybee" and symbolizing industry.) For information, facts, and figures on many aspects of Utah life, the *Atlas of Utah* edited by Wayne L. Wahlquist (Provo, UT: Brigham Young University Press, 1981) is outstanding. Full color illustrations, maps, and charts offer data on everything from flora and fauna to major fast food chains.

Index to Recipes